YOU CAN DRAW Anything!

grab a pencil and make your mark on the world of art!

Flick through the pages of this book to find the things you want to draw, then follow the steps to transform simple shapes into magical masterpieces.

But don't just stop there! Be inspired to draw everything around you, using the tips and techniques you pick up along the way.

And remember, the more you practise, the more your confidence will grow and the more you'll be ready to DRAW ANYTHING!

This edition published by Parragon Books Ltd in 2016

Parragon Books Ltd
Chartist House
15–17 Trim Street
Bath BA1 1HA, UK
www.parragon.com

Illustrated by Si Clark, Paula Franco, Alex Hedworth, Steve Horrocks, Julie Ingham, Tom McGrath, David Shephard and Yasuko
Photographs from Shutterstock, Inc.

ISBN 978-1-4748-0248-2
Printed in China

YOU CAN DRAW Anything!

PaRragon

Bath · New York · Cologne · Melbourne · Delhi
Hong Kong · Shenzhen · Singapore

CONTENTS

MATERIALS

ALL YOU REALLY NEED TO DRAW IS A PENCIL AND SOME PAPER, BUT OTHER MATERIALS CAN HELP TRANSPORT YOUR ARTWORK TO ANOTHER LEVEL.

PAPER
Different kinds of paper and pencils can dramatically alter the appearance of your drawing.

Copy paper is great for sharp pencil lines, cartridge paper gives a softer effect and watercolour paper keeps the colour of ink and watercolour paints brilliant. To copy or print objects, use transparent (tracing) paper to transfer images onto plain paper.

ERASERS
Rub away mistakes or unwanted guidelines with an eraser. Also use it to create highlights by sweeping it across your drawing.

PENCILS
For thin, fine pencil lines, choose an H (hard) pencil or an HB pencil (a little softer). For shading and blending, go for B (soft). These come in numbered degrees of hard and soft.

PEN AND INK
For line art, to go over outlines or to make objects stand out from their backgrounds, try a cartridge pen, dip pen and ink or even a fine-tipped brush and ink.

WATERCOLOUR AND COLOURED PENCILS

Watercolour pencils use water to help blend different colours and shades together. Regular coloured pencils are great for creating animal fur and feathery textures.

PAINTS AND BRUSHES

For a soft, blending effect, try watercolour paint and for a heavier, more opaque finish, try gouache paint. For a thick, vibrant appearance, try acrylic or opaque paint – it's great for smooth, solid objects. You can also create these painting techniques digitally.

Experiment with round brushes for washes and general painting, pointed brushes for fine detail and flat brushes to sweep an even amount of colour on bigger areas.

CRAYONS AND PENS

Crayons are great for adding texture to your picture...

... and felt pens make objects pop from their backgrounds. You can also use felt or marker pens to outline your work and draw attention to individual elements of your drawing.

TECHNIQUES

EXPERIMENT WITH DIFFERENT DRAWING TECHNIQUES TO FIND THE RIGHT APPROACH FOR YOU AND YOUR WORK OF ART!

SHAPES AND SYMMETRY

Break objects down into simple shapes to help get the proportions right from the start. Then draw around the shapes to join them together for the object's outline.

Add a centre guideline for symmetrical objects and mirror what you draw on each side.

LINES AND SHADING

For shaded areas, rub the side of a pencil on paper with varied pressure or use the tip of the pencil to draw lines - the closer the lines, the darker the shading.

DEPTH, DISTANCE AND DIMENSION

Make your drawing appear realistic by turning basic shapes into 3D objects and using perspective to provide a clear foreground and background in your picture. Objects in the foreground are bigger and normally brighter.

light source

horizon line

vanishing point

Shadows also suggest depth and distance. The higher the light source, the shorter the shadow. Use a light source and vanishing point for accurate shadows.

REFLECTION AND LIGHT

To give an impression of glass, start with darker shades first and leave the lighter areas white.

To highlight shiny areas, sweep an eraser over your pencil work, or wash paint away with a brush. Add angled lines on reflected areas for more depth.

ACTION AND MOTION

Movement can bring your drawings to life. Simply angle hair and clothes for action poses, and create motion lines or smudgy paint marks on fast-moving objects.

BRUSH STROKES AND COLOUR

There are different techniques to use when colouring. Long, sweeping brush strokes will create a smooth appearance, while a quick jab of the brush (or stippling) adds texture. Dot painting gives a stylistic pattern-like picture.

Use complementary colours (red and green) or contrasting colours (red and yellow) to complete your masterpiece.

DRAWING PEOPLE IS A GOOD SKILL FOR ARTISTS TO DEVELOP. BREAK THEM DOWN INTO SIMPLE STEPS.

Use a reference photo of a friend or someone famous to help you get your pose right.

1
SKETCH A STICK FIGURE TO GET THE BASIC POSE. THINK ABOUT WHETHER YOU WANT IT TO BE RELAXED OR DYNAMIC.

2
DRAW A ROUGH OUTLINE OF THE BODY SHAPE AROUND YOUR GUIDE. FOCUS ON GETTING THE PROPORTIONS RIGHT.

3
SKETCH SURFACE DETAIL ON THE CLOTHES, DRAWING JAGGED LINES FOR THE FOLDS. ADD FACIAL DETAILS TOO.

Experiment with different hairstyles and clothing on your people.

1
AS ABOVE, SKETCH A SIMPLE STICK FIGURE. WORK FROM A PHOTO OR GET SOMEONE TO POSE FOR YOU, IF YOU CAN.

2
OUTLINE THE SHAPES OF THE HAIR AND CLOTHES. THIS POSE IS RELAXED, SO ONE SIDE LOOKS A LITTLE LOWER THAN THE OTHER.

3
WORK ON ADDING MORE SURFACE DETAIL. MAKE SURE THE GIRL'S EXPRESSION MATCHES HER LAID-BACK POSE.

5

ADD SOME SCENERY IN THE BACKGROUND, THEN GO OVER YOUR DRAWING IN BLACK INK. USE WATERCOLOURS IN DIFFERENT SHADES TO CREATE A FEELING OF DEPTH.

Use pale washes and muted colours for the background. These will help your figure stand out.

4

REFINE YOUR PENCIL LINES AND CONCENTRATE ON ADDING FINE DETAIL. USE SHORT LINES TO ADD PATCHES OF SHADING FOR THE SHADOWY AREAS.

5

SKETCH SOME SCENERY AND THEN INK IN YOUR DRAWING. CHOOSE COLOURS FOR YOUR FIGURE THAT HELP HER TO STAND OUT FROM THE BACKGROUND.

Add subtle areas of shading when you colour your picture. It really helps sell the idea that the figure is in 3D.

4

NOW ADD THE FINE DETAILS. THINK ABOUT THE WAY THE FOLDS IN THE JEANS FALL, THEN SKETCH IN CREASE LINES. THESE WILL HELP EMPHASIZE THE OVERALL POSE. SHADE IN THE HAIR.

WALKING AWAY

LOTS OF PEOPLE STRUGGLE TO DRAW BACKS OF PEOPLE AND HEADS. LEARN HOW HERE!

Draw a centre line, then add a circle on top for the head. Sketch the ears, neck and shoulders beneath it, like this.

Create a shaggy shape around the head for hair. Add wavy lines inside it. Then draw two curved lines for the T-shirt.

When colouring, use light and dark shading on the hair to give it depth and movement.

Try drawing the whole body from the back. Create creases on the hood and jacket, and colour the drawing in light and dark shades.

A hand slung casually in the pocket gives a faceless character a bit of personality.

Sketch one leg bent with the trainer upturned for a walking pose.

For a ponytail, sketch curved lines leading to a semi-circular shape. Then draw loose longer strands down the back.

To create soft curls, sketch long wavy lines, flowing in different directions.

Start a bun like a ponytail, but draw short curved lines for the actual shape of the bun.

Add fine details to clothes and bags, like belts and buckles. Then create more meaning to your artwork. Hidden arm gestures and matching leg and feet positions suggest these characters know each other and are perfectly in tune.

13

MOST THINGS CAN BE BROKEN DOWN INTO SHAPES. LEARN TO DRAW THE BASICS HERE.

CIRCLE TO SPHERE

Start with a simple circle. Draw it by hand or with a compass.

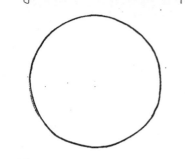

Decide where the light source is coming from, then add shading on the opposite side of the circle, following the curved line.

Add colour, then create a circular highlight with an eraser to make a sphere. Paint darker marks on the sphere for texture.

SQUARE TO CUBE

Draw a square, making sure each side is equal in length.

Sketch or trace an overlapping square on top of the original, as shown. Draw lines to join the two squares together.

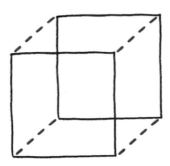

For a 3D effect, sketch darker shadows on the side and front of the cube, with lighter shades on top.

TRIANGLE TO PYRAMID

First sketch an equal-sided triangle, like this.

Draw a short diagonal line out from the bottom right corner and a longer line linking up to the tip of the triangle.

Create depth with your shading and colour by making the side of the pyramid darker than the front.

CONE AND CYLINDER

For a cone, draw an oval base, then a line leading up from the middle. Add lines down the sides, connecting the top to the base.

To make a cylinder shape, sketch two parallel ovals on their sides, joined together by two parallel vertical lines and shading.

DRAWING WITH SHAPES

Use a combination of simple shapes for more complex drawings.

Try a cube-shaped robot with cylinders for the head, legs and arms, and cone-shaped hands.

A tennis ball is easy when you know how to draw a sphere!

Design your own can of pop from a cylinder.

3D

MAKE YOUR DRAWINGS EXTRA REALISTIC BY DRAWING IN THREE DIMENSIONS: LENGTH, DEPTH AND WIDTH. START BY LEARNING TO DRAW A BUILDING IN THIS WAY.

1 SKETCH RECTANGLES FOR EACH FRONT-FACING SECTION OF THE BUILDING, AS SHOWN. ADD THE BASIC SHAPE OF THE STEPS.

2 NOW DRAW THE SAME SHAPES FURTHER AWAY, AT A DIFFERENT ANGLE, LIKE THIS.

3 JOIN THE CORNERS OF THE REPEATING SHAPES TOGETHER FOR THE 3D EFFECT.

4

TO ADD DETAIL, SKETCH SQUARES AND RECTANGLES FOR WINDOWS, AND CURVED LINES FOR PIPES. ADD OVALS TO THE NECK OF THE BUILDING.

Create 3D window sills using long 3D rectangles.

3D STEPS

Create an outline of the steps, as shown. Repeat the step shape further away. Then sketch parallel lines to join each step together. Add light and dark shading, and colour the steps in.

5 CHOOSE THE DIRECTION OF YOUR LIGHT SOURCE. THEN KEEP THE PARTS OF THE BUILDING FACING THE LIGHT BRIGHTER THAN THE AREAS ON THE OTHER SIDE, WHICH SHOULD BE DARKER. ADD COLOUR TO FINISH YOUR 3D BUILDING.

Sketchy lines give the walls of the building a rough-looking texture.

Add diagonal lines on the windows to give an impression of glass.

PORTRAIT

1 SKETCH AN ANGLED OVAL SHAPE. DRAW A CURVED, VERTICAL LINE AND THREE HORIZONTAL GUIDELINES, LINING UP WITH THE EAR AS SHOWN. ADD NECK LINES.

2 USE THE GUIDELINES TO POSITION THE FACIAL FEATURES. NOTICE HOW THE EYES ARE LEVEL WITH THE TOP OF THE EAR AND THE MOUTH WITH THE BOTTOM.

5 DEFINE THE HAIR SHAPE, PARTICULARLY WHERE IT MEETS THE COLLAR. ADD LIGHT PATCHES OF SHADING FOR TEXTURE. ADD CLOTHING DETAIL.

6 WORK OUT WHERE THE SHADOWS SHOULD BE AND SHADE IN THOSE AREAS. REFINE THE DETAIL OF THE EYES, NOSE, MOUTH AND HAIR.

Keep your wrist relaxed as you draw. It will make it easier to sketch nice smooth curves.

3 SKETCH THE OUTLINE OF THE HAIR USING LONG, SWEEPING CURVES. REMEMBER JUST TO FOCUS ON THE OVERALL SHAPE AT THIS STAGE.

4 ADD A LITTLE MORE DETAIL TO THE FACIAL FEATURES AND USE MORE CURVED LINES TO SHOW HOW THE HAIR FALLS ACROSS THE FACE.

Stick with a light pencil until you're happy with the overall shape of your portrait.

7 PAINT YOUR PORTRAIT USING WATERCOLOURS. CHOOSE A BASE TONE FOR THE SKIN, THEN ADD BOTH LIGHTER AND DARKER SHADES ON TOP TO EMPHASIZE THE SHAPES OF THE FEATURES.

Try to keep your painting technique fairly loose. It will help give your final portrait more life and character!

SHADOWS

LEARN ABOUT LIGHT SOURCES AND THE SHADOWS THEY CREATE TO TURN YOUR FLAT DRAWINGS INTO REALISTIC 3D.

ADDING SHADOWS IN PERSPECTIVE CAN LOOK TRICKY, BUT THESE SIMPLE TIPS WILL HELP YOU LEARN TECHNIQUES YOU CAN USE AGAIN AND AGAIN.

light source

Mark a vanishing point in the distance. Draw guidelines to sketch a cuboid shape in perspective.

vanishing point

Now add a light source above the cuboid. Draw lines leading down from the middle of the light to the far corners of the cuboid.

For the shadow, shade the areas where the light source lines meet the vanishing point lines.

A light source positioned higher up will result in a shorter shadow, while a light lower down gives a longer shadow.

SHADING EFFECTS

With a soft B pencil apply pressure to the paper, gradually easing off towards the end for a dark-to-light effect.

To shade using crosshatching, draw lines in opposing diagonal directions over the area you want to darken.

20

CASTING SHADOWS

USE A SIMILAR TECHNIQUE TO CREATE EFFECTIVE SHADOWS IN OTHER DRAWINGS, LIKE A TREE, HOUSE OR EVEN PEOPLE!

light source

HOUSE OF DARKNESS
Sketch one shape at a time for this tricky shadow, using the vanishing point lines to help. Ensure the light source lines touch the corners of the house, as shown.

SHADY TREE
Draw lines from the light source across the tips of the tree to the ground. Use these lines to roughly draw the length and width of the tree's shadow.

light source

FLOOR SILHOUETTE
Apply the same method to create a shadow on the ground. You can work out the length of the shadow with a triangle, as shown.

SHADOWS ON THE WALL
Cast a big wall shadow, using a right-angled triangle to help work out its size. Bend the shadow where the floor hits the wall.

light source

21

THE CITY

CREATE A CITY LANDSCAPE USING ONLY LINE ART: A COMBINATION OF DIFFERENT LINE STYLES.

START WITH A 3D OUTLINE OF YOUR LANDSCAPE. USE A MIXTURE OF RECTANGULAR, TRIANGULAR AND CYLINDRICAL SHAPES, LIKE THIS.

Apply different line effects on each building for a cool, varied city look. Try crosshatching on one side of the building and a mixture of horizontal and vertical lines on another.

INK LINE STYLES

Horizontal lines highlight the width of a building and give a sense of space.

Vertical lines elongate buildings, leading the eye up to the sky.

Crosshatching is overlapping lines in opposite directions to create shading.

Build up cross-hatching for flat black, going over and over the same area.

Lines drawn close together give a darker shading effect than those drawn further apart. For more depth, add flat black shading to buildings in the background.

FLOWER POWER

FLOWERS COME IN ALL SHAPES AND COLOURS. TRY THESE TECHNIQUES IN YOUR OWN FLORAL DRAWINGS.

1

TO DRAW A POPPY, FIRST SKETCH THE HEAD USING SIMPLE, WAVY SHAPES FOR THE PETALS, AS SHOWN.

2

DRAW A RECTANGLE SHAPE IN THE MIDDLE OF THE HEAD. ADD SMALL THIN STICKS WITH TINY LEAF-LIKE SHAPES ON TOP.

3

LIGHTLY DRAW LINES ON THE PETALS FOR TEXTURE. ADD TWO LONG LINES BENEATH THE FLOWER HEAD TO CREATE A STEM.

Sketch borders and crease lines in the petals. Then use complementary colours to finish this pretty plant.

Draw a droopy stalk with an oval-shaped bud to add to the scene.

4

GO OVER YOUR DRAWING WITH INK.
RUB AWAY ANY PENCIL MARKS AND
COLOUR THE POPPY HEAD A DEEP RED.

For a rose in bloom, start with
small petals in the centre and
make them bigger as you work
your way out.

Use vibrant colours to finish your
blossoms. The brighter the better!

FRUIT BOWL

A MUST-LEARN FOR ANY BUDDING ARTIST!

1 USING A PENCIL, DRAW A SIMPLE BOWL SHAPE SIDE ON. GIVE IT A ROUNDED BRIM WITH A SHALLOW BASE AT THE BOTTOM.

2 LOOSELY SKETCH THE SHAPES OF DIFFERENT FRUITS.

Pick a single colour for the bowl, with a darker shade for the areas in shadow. Or make up your own design!

3

START REFINING YOUR OUTLINES, ADDING SMALLER FRUIT SHAPES HERE AND THERE TOO. RUB OUT YOUR ROUGH GUIDELINES.

4 DECIDE WHERE THE LIGHT IS COMING FROM IN YOUR DRAWING, THEN ADD SOME SHADING TO THE AREAS THAT ARE IN SHADOW.

Light source

6

WHEN COLOURING YOUR DRAWING, THINK ABOUT HOW THE SHINY FRUIT PEEL WILL REFLECT THE LIGHT. CREATE HIGHLIGHTS BY LEAVING SOME AREAS WHITE.

Shiny objects will slightly reflect the colour of whatever is near to them. So, add a red tinge to the fruit that's next to the bright red apple.

5 REALLY WORK UP THE FRUIT SHAPES AND FOCUS ON MORE SUBTLE SHADING TO MAKE THE FRUIT LOOK MORE ROUNDED. THIS WILL ALSO HELP ADD DEPTH TO YOUR PICTURE.

The Taj Mahal was built around 1653 in Agra, India, and is an admired work of art! Find a photo of this famous landmark for your drawing reference.

1

START WITH SIMPLE SHAPES TO BUILD YOUR MONUMENT: LIGHTLY SKETCH A HORIZONTAL LINE, TWO VERTICAL LINES, THREE RECTANGLES AND AN OVAL, AS SHOWN. USE A RULER IF YOU LIKE.

 # TAJ MAHAL

Work on smaller sections at a time to help you focus on the line work.

4

START WORKING UP THE FEATURES SUCH AS ARCHES, DOORS, WINDOWS AND PILLARS. USE A FINE INK PEN TO DRAW OVER THE TOP OF YOUR PENCIL SKETCH.

5

USE A MIXTURE OF TINY CRISS-CROSS LINES, OVALS, DOME SHAPES AND CIRCLES TO CREATE THE MONUMENT'S DECORATIVE DETAIL. RUB AWAY ANY PENCIL MARKS.

2

DRAW A DOME SHAPE AROUND THE OVAL, THEN USE A RULER TO ADD SMALLER RECTANGLES TO THE BUILDING, AS SHOWN. NOW DRAW TWO MORE VERTICAL LINES ON THE OUTER EDGES.

3

SKETCH FOUR SHORT HORIZONTAL LINES ON EACH OF THE FOUR VERTICAL LINES TO PREPARE FOR DRAWING THE PILLARS. DRAW CURVED LINES WITHIN THE DOME SHAPE, THEN ADD TWO SMALL DOMES ON EITHER SIDE.

6

FINALLY, ADD A WASH OF COLOUR INK OR WATERCOLOUR PAINT OVER THE MONUMENT AND SKY. DRAW THREE SIMPLE BIRD SHAPES WITH YOUR PEN TO FINISH.

Use light and dark shades to suggest shadow and depth.

PROFILES

1

DRAW A LARGE SQUARE AND DIVIDE WITH HORIZONTAL LINES AND A LINE DOWN THE MIDDLE, AS SHOWN. SKETCH AN OVAL FOR THE HEAD AND A POINTED SHAPE FOR THE JAW.

2

USING YOUR GUIDES, DRAW BASIC SHAPES FOR THE EYES, EYE SOCKETS, NOSE, MOUTH AND EARS. NOTICE HOW THE EYE IS SET BACK A LITTLE FROM THE BRIDGE OF THE NOSE.

3

REFINE THE SHAPES OF THE VARIOUS FACIAL FEATURES A LITTLE. ADD A JAGGED LINE FOR THE HAIRLINE, RUNNING FROM THE TOP OF THE FOREHEAD DOWN TO THE EAR.

4

RUB OUT YOUR GUIDELINES AND WORK ON THE FINER DETAILS. DRAW THE SHAPE OF THE HAIR AND ADD DETAIL TO THE EYES, NOSE AND MOUTH.

5

USING A PEN OR SHARP PENCIL, GIVE THE EYEBROWS AND HAIR MORE TEXTURE. MAKE LOTS OF FINE LINES USING SHORT STROKES.

6

PAINT THE FACE WITH A MIX OF RED, WHITE AND BROWN TO MAKE THE RIGHT SKIN COLOUR. USE DIFFERENT TONES TO SHOW CONTOURS OF THE FACE, AS WELL AS AREAS OF LIGHT AND SHADE.

To make the skin look smooth, try to fade gradually between the lighter and darker tones.

PROFILE FEATURES

NOSES

Have fun drawing different nose shapes. Perhaps you could ask your family and friends if you can sketch them in profile?

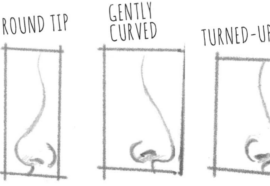

ROUND TIP GENTLY CURVED TURNED-UP TIP STRAIGHT CROOKED

HEADS

People's head shapes can vary a lot too. Notice the differences in bone structure, and how someone's hairstyle also changes the overall shape of their head.

BAGS

BAGS FOR GUYS

TODAY THERE ARE MORE BAG STYLES FOR BOYS THAN EVER BEFORE! BE INSPIRED BY FASHION MAGAZINES OR GO ONLINE FOR THE LATEST LOOKS. TRY DRAWING A BAG AT AN ANGLE TO GIVE IT MORE INTEREST.

SATCHEL

Draw an angled rectangle with a side panel for depth. Add a strap, side pocket and skateboarder shape.

Use tones of the same colour for depth. You could also try a shorter flap with straps and buckles for a vintage look.

RUCKSACK

ZIPPED MESSENGER BAG

SCHOOL BAG

It's all in the extras with this bag! Draw a wobbly rectangle, then sketch pockets, straps, buckles, tassels and a handle.

For the zip, draw two long horizontal lines joined by lots of tiny vertical lines, then add a small rectangular pull.

Too cool for school? Use weirdly complementary colours to create an eye-catching effect that grabs attention.

TOTE, HANDBAG, SATCHEL... WHAT WILL IT BE? LEARN TO DRAW THE VARIOUS STYLES THEN TRY OUT DIFFERENT PATTERNS FOR EXTRA DETAIL.

TOTE

Draw a square, then add two arches for the handle. Draw dashed lines for stitching, a pocket and some stylin' stars.

Make your star pattern pop by colouring the stars and pocket in lighter or darker shades of the main bag colour.

Have fun creating unique details like this clutch bag's asymmetrical flap. Stick to a basic colour for a sophisticated design.

BUCKLED HANDBAG

SATCHEL HANDBAG

CARPET BAG

Draw chunky straps and buckles for easy-going elegance. Add a cute pocket and clasp as a finishing touch.

Create clasps and keyrings out of circles and rectangles, making an ordinary design feel a little more special.

A carpet bag doesn't need a carpet pattern! Draw lines going down and across to achieve a chequered look.

DOGS, DOGS, DOGS!

FAT OR FURRY, SHORT OR SHAGGY - HERE'S HOW TO DRAW THE PERFECT POOCH!

1 SKETCH A BIG OVAL FOR THE BODY, WITH A ROUGH CIRCLE FOR THE HEAD. USE CURVED AND STRAIGHT LINES TO SKETCH THE LEGS AND TAIL.

2 DRAW TRIANGLES FOR THE EARS AND OVALS FOR THE EYES AND NOSE. FLESH OUT THE SHAPES OF THE LEGS, PAWS AND TAIL.

3 START ADDING DETAIL. DRAW EXTRA LINES ON THE FACE FOR THE DOG'S WRINKLY SKIN. ADD THE MOUTH AND A COLLAR.

4 REFINE YOUR PENCIL LINES, THEN USE SHORT PENCIL STROKES TO CREATE A FUR TEXTURE. ADD LOTS OF PENCIL DOTS AROUND THE MUZZLE.

5 PAINT THE COAT A PALE BROWN, ADDING PATCHES OF GREY TO THE EARS AND MUZZLE AREA. PICK OUT THE COLLAR IN A BRIGHT, CONTRASTING COLOUR.

Draw a dinner bowl or other doggy object to add interest to your picture.

NOW TRY SOME OF THESE DOGS AND STYLES!

FUR AND HAIR

Use fine, squiggly lines to draw the texture of a terrier's shaggy coat. Use shorter pencil strokes for its furry face.

TERRIER

POODLE

Use rounded shapes and tiny pencil strokes to create the neatly groomed outline and look of a poodle. Colour using white and off-white tones.

MARKINGS

Draw large patches on the dog's body and add shading using crosshatching.

BASSET HOUND

BULL DOG

Use short pencil strokes for these markings. Follow the contour of the body, emphasizing its shape.

SILHOUETTES

Practise sketching dogs in silhouette. It'll help you get better at drawing different poses.

SCOTTY DOG

CHIHUAHUA

Silhouettes help you think about different doggy shapes. This one's ears are huge compared to its body!

MIRRORS AND GLASS

LEARN HOW TO CREATE MIRRORED AND REFLECTIVE SURFACES TO ADD DIMENSION AND DEPTH TO YOUR DRAWINGS.

1
SKETCH AN OVAL, THEN DRAW A FRAME AROUND IT, LIKE THIS. ADD DARK SHADING ON ONE SIDE OF THE MIRROR.

When creating the appearance of glass, it's best to start with the darkest shades first.

2
SKETCH CIRCLES AND SWIRLY LINES ON THE FRAME FOR DECORATION. NOW ADD A LIGHTER LAYER OF BLUE SHADING ON THE MIRROR.

Use the eraser to add highlights and contrast.

3
SWEEP AN ERASER ACROSS THE MIRROR TO GIVE AN IMPRESSION OF REFLECTED LIGHT.

4
ADD LIGHTER SHADING TO THE MIRROR WITH A SWIRLING MOTION. DRAW DIAGONAL LINES FOR A MORE 3D EFFECT.

Colour the frame using light and dark circular strokes for a shiny appearance.

REFLECTION

DRAW A MIRROR THEN ADD THE REFLECTION OF YOUR CHARACTER INSIDE IT. SKETCH THE BACK OF THE CHARACTER OUTSIDE OF THE MIRROR.

Add light and dark shading to the mirror, using the same technique as before. Colour the reflected character slightly lighter than the actual one.

GLASS

USE A SIMILAR APPROACH WHEN DRAWING GLASS-BASED OBJECTS, LIKE A MARBLE OR A DRINKING GLASS.

Make the positions in the reflection and the real object match as well as possible.

1

FOR THE MARBLE, SKETCH A CIRCLE, THEN DRAW SEVERAL SWIRLY LINES ACROSS THE CENTRE, AS SHOWN.

2

ADD LINES AND SHADING AROUND THE MARBLE AND ON EACH SHAPE INSIDE IT. USE AN ERASER TO CREATE HIGHLIGHTS ON THE GLASS.

1

DRAW A CYLINDER SHAPE FOR THE GLASS, WITH A FLATTENED OVAL SHAPE IN THE MIDDLE FOR THE WATER. ADD THE STRAW.

2

USE DARK SHADING AROUND THE BASE OF THE GLASS AND TO CREATE VERTICAL LINES FOR THE RIDGES. ADD HIGHLIGHTS WITH AN ERASER.

Draw a wobbly straw outline beneath the water for a distorted effect.

37

WEATHER

DIFFERENT ELEMENTS CAN GIVE THE SAME SCENE A VERY DIFFERENT FEEL!

RAIN

DRAW LONG SLOPING LINES TO CREATE RAIN. PAINT THEM A LIGHT COLOUR TO MAKE THEM STAND OUT AGAINST DARK STORM CLOUDS.

PAINT THE TREE AND GRASS WITH DARK TONES.

DRAW RIPPLES ON WATER BY SKETCHING CONCENTRIC CIRCLES THAT RADIATE OUTWARDS AND MERGE INTO EACH OTHER.

WIND

THE WIND MAKES THE TREES, FLOWERS AND GRASS BEND IN THE SAME DIRECTION.

USER BRIGHTER COLOURS FOR THE TREE AND GRASS FOR A SUNNY BUT BLUSTERY DAY.

DRAW LEAVES DANCING IN THE AIR TO GIVE THE IMPRESSION OF A STRONG BREEZE. GIVE SOME OF THEM WAVY TRAILS TO ADD MOVEMENT.

ELECTRIC STORM

USE ZIG-ZAGS TO DRAW A BOLT OF LIGHTNING. NOTICE HOW IT SPLITS INTO FORKS AS IT GETS NEAR THE GROUND.

THE WHOLE SCENE SHOULD BE DARK EXCEPT THE LIGHTNING AND REFLECTIONS.

LIGHTNING REFLECTIONS CAN EASILY BE SEEN ON THE SURFACE OF WATER. TO GET THIS EFFECT, SIMPLY DRAW THE LIGHTNING'S MIRROR IMAGE.

SNOW AND ICE

DRAW ICICLES USING LONG, OVERLAPPING 'V' SHAPES AND SHADING.

THE WHOLE SCENE IS BRIGHT WITH LIGHT REFLECTING OFF SNOW.

USE CURVED LINES TO DRAW MOUNDS OF SNOW. PAINT SHADOWY AREAS IN BLUE RATHER THAN GREY TO REFLECT THE BLUE SKY ABOVE.

HAND

Draw a horizontal line halfway up the hand to help you position the thumb correctly.

1

FOR THE KNUCKLES, SKETCH A ROOF SHAPE WITH THE POINT POSITIONED AS SHOWN. FOR THE HAND, DRAW BULGING SIDES AND A HORIZONTAL LINE.

2/3   1/3

2

ADD VERTICAL LINES FOR THE WRIST BONE, A SEMI-CIRCLE FOR THE THUMB AND SHORT GUIDELINES ON THE KNUCKLES FOR THE FINGERS.

1/2

1/2

3

SKETCH GUIDELINES FOR THE FINGERS AND THEIR JOINTS, USING THE KEY FOR SCALE BELOW. DRAW LINES FOR THE THUMB AND A CIRCLE FOR ITS JOINT.

4

DRAW AN OUTLINE AROUND THE HAND TO JOIN THE SHAPES TOGETHER, LIKE THIS. LOOK AT YOUR OWN HAND FOR REFERENCE.

5

RUB AWAY THE GUIDELINES AND ADD COLOUR AND SHADING. ADD OVAL-SHAPED NAILS AND CREASE LINES ON THE FINGER JOINTS.

FINGER JOINT KEY:

1/3
1/2   2/3

1/2

1/2

Each finger should be as long as the distance from its base to the wrist.

Align the thumb joint with the line from the knuckle of the index finger.

40

STRIKE A POSE!

TRY EXPERIMENTING WITH DIFFERENT HAND POSITIONS AND LEARN HOW TO ALTER THE SKIN, JOINTS AND MUSCLE TONE WITH EACH NEW SHAPE YOU MAKE.

DRAW THE PALM IN A SIMILAR WAY TO THE BACK OF THE HAND BUT HIGHLIGHT THE MUSCLES WITH CURVED LINES AND SHADING.

FOR A CLENCHED FIST, DRAW A BUMPY LINE WHERE THE JOINTS PUSH TOGETHER. ADD LINES AND SHADING ON THE PALM TO SUGGEST WRINKLED SKIN.

CREATE A SIDE-ON VIEW, WITH THE MIDDLE FINGER HIDING THE SMALLER DIGITS BEHIND IT. GIVE THE HAND A SLIGHTLY CURVED SPADE SHAPE.

TO DRAW AN OPENED-OUT HAND, REFER TO MODELS AND PICTURES OF SKELETONS. A GOOD UNDERSTANDING OF HOW BONES AND JOINTS WORK TOGETHER WILL HELP WHEN YOU GO ON TO DRAW PEOPLE AND ANIMALS.

FOR A POINTING POSE, IMAGINE THE FINGERS ARE BOX-SHAPED RATHER THAN ROUND. VIEW THE JOINTS LIKE DOOR HINGES. IF YOU KNOW WHERE THEY BEND, YOU CAN POSITION THE FINGERS MORE ACCURATELY.

FLAMINGOS

1

START WITH CIRCLES FOR THE HEAD AND BODY, STRAIGHT LINES FOR THE LEGS, AN 'S' SHAPE FOR THE NECK AND TRIANGLES FOR THE FEET. ADD A HOOKED, POINTY BEAK.

2

JOIN THE BASIC SHAPES TOGETHER WITH A STRONGER OUTLINE. USE STEP 1 AS A GUIDE TO HELP YOU GET THE PROPORTIONS RIGHT.

3

ADD MORE DETAIL TO YOUR DRAWING: AN EYE, A NOSTRIL ON THE BEAK, FEATHERY WINGS AND WEBBED FEET, AS SHOWN.

1

SKETCH A BABY FLAMINGO IN A SIMILAR WAY TO THE ADULT ONE, BUT MAKE THE SHAPES SMALLER AND SHORTER, APART FROM THE FEET.

2

GO AROUND THE GUIDELINES, AS BEFORE, BUT THIS TIME MAKE THE LEGS A BIT THICKER AND THE WINGS STUBBIER. ADD IN FACIAL FEATURES.

4

CAREFULLY RUB AWAY YOUR GUIDELINES TO REVEAL YOUR FLAMINGO DRAWING.

5

COLOUR WITH WATERCOLOUR PENCILS. CREATE A FEATHERY TEXTURE WITH THE DIRECTION OF YOUR STROKES AND A 3D EFFECT WITH LIGHT AND DARK SHADES.

Try drawing a flying flamingo with wide, open wings and a straight, horizontal body line.

Try another flamingo pose, with the head and neck down. Add bulrushes to build up the setting.

3

RUB AWAY YOUR GUIDELINES TO LEAVE JUST THE OUTLINE AND FEATURES OF YOUR BABY FLAMINGO.

4

APPLY LIGHT GREY SHADING ON THE BODY. CREATE THE EFFECT OF FLUFFY FEATHERS BY USING SHORT PAINT STROKES. COLOUR THE LEGS, FEET AND BEAK WITH LIGHT AND DARK SHADING.

EYES

MASTER THIS FACIAL FEATURE THEN CREATE ALMOST ANY MOOD OR EMOTION YOU LIKE JUST BY VARYING THE SHAPE!

FRONT-ON

1
DRAW A CURVED LINE AND BIG CIRCLE AS GUIDES. DRAW A POINTED EYEBALL AND ARC WITHIN THE CIRCLE.

2
RUB OUT THE BIG CIRCLE AND LINE. DRAW ANOTHER CIRCLE FOR THE IRIS AND A SMALLER ONE FOR THE PUPIL.

3
USE PENCIL FLICKS TO DRAW EYELASHES. SHADE AROUND THE EDGE OF THE IRIS AND ADD A CIRCULAR HIGHLIGHT.

4
TO PAINT THE IRIS, USE DIFFERENT SHADES OF THE SAME COLOUR TO SHOW THE EYE'S REFLECTIVE QUALITY.

IN PROFILE

1
DRAW A BIG CIRCLE FOR THE EYEBALL, BUT THIS TIME SKETCH THE VISIBLE PART AS A BIG TRIANGLE.

2
DRAW THE UPPER EYELID, WHICH STICKS OUT A LITTLE. ADD A CURVE TO FORM THE IRIS.

3
RUB OUT THE EYEBALL GUIDELINES AND SKETCH SOME EYELASHES. ADD A THIN OVAL FOR THE PUPIL.

4
ADD PENCIL SHADING TO DEFINE THE SHAPE OF THE EYE SOCKET. PAINT THE IRIS AS BEFORE IN DIFFERENT SHADES OF THE SAME COLOUR.

Creating expressions

SURPRISE

Draw the eye wide open so that the iris is fully visible. The eyebrow needs to be raised quite high above the eye.

ANGER

Draw the eyelids much closer together and add crease lines to show tension. Sketch the inner part of the eyebrow much closer to the eye.

HAPPY

Draw the lids close together, but make the lower lid slightly curved, as shown. Add some curved crease lines around the eye and a relaxed brow.

SAD

Draw the eyelids so that most of the iris is visible. Sketch the inner part of the eyebrow high up, to convey a frown. Add a dripping tear, too!

CLOUDS

THERE ARE LOTS OF DIFFERENT TYPES OF CLOUD.
LEARN DIFFERENT TECHNIQUES TO DRAW THEM ALL!

CUMULUS

1

Draw uneven, overlapping circle shapes, then add wavy horizontal lines for the base of the clouds.

2

Paint the shape of the cloud in a bluey-grey colour. Then add white and blue reflections from the sun and sky. Paint shadows underneath in warmer hues.

LENTICULARIS

Sketch thin oval shapes piled up on top of each other. Paint the darkest part first, then add highlights with opaque or acrylic paint.

CIRROCUMULUS
Use quick, short jabs or strokes (called stippling) of transparent paint with a rough flat brush to create flecks of clouds. Layer the paint into thicker and thinner areas.

CIRRUS
With a thin brush, gradually build up layers of transparent paint. Fade out the ends to give a wispy cloud effect.

NACREOUS
Paint the background white, then sweep layers of transparent paint over the top with a round brush for a coloured 'mother of pearl' effect.

CUMULONIMBUS
Layer up lots of cumulus-like circles into a big towering structure, which mushrooms out over the top. Use dark paint to make ominous, gloomy-looking shadows.

47

RUNNER

1
DRAW OVALS FOR THE HEAD AND FEET, LINES FOR THE NECK, BODY, ARMS AND LEGS AND CIRCLES FOR THE HANDS AND JOINTS, AS SHOWN.

Add guidelines for the eyes and nose.

2
SKETCH A MIXTURE OF CIRCLES AND ROUGH SAUSAGE SHAPES TO BUILD UP THE LIMBS. DRAW CURVED LINES FOR THE NECK AND TORSO.

3
JOIN THE LIMB SHAPES TOGETHER WITH MORE DISTINCT OUTLINES TO BRING OUT THE CURVES AND CONTOURS OF THE BODY.

Draw a triangle for the nose.

4
SKETCH SMALL LINES ON THE ARMS AND LEGS TO SUGGEST MUSCLE TONE. START ADDING IN THE HANDS AND FACIAL FEATURES.

5
NOW FOCUS ON THE FINER DETAILS. DRAW THE RUNNER'S CLOTHES, TRAINERS, HAIR, EYES AND EYEBROWS.

6 DARKEN THE OUTLINES AND ADD SHADING TO GIVE YOUR DRAWING DEPTH, DIMENSION AND MUSCLE DEFINITION.

Lightly curved lines around the limbs add motion and movement to your drawing.

Shading on the ground suggests your runner is in mid-stride and mid-air.

7

USE BRIGHT COLOURS TO HELP YOUR RUNNER STAND OUT FROM A PALE BACKGROUND.

BUTTERFLIES

BUTTERFLY WING PATTERNS CAN LOOK COMPLEX BUT THEY ARE EASY TO DRAW IF YOU USE SYMMETRY. TRY THESE THEN CREATE YOUR OWN!

1

START BY DRAWING A CIRCLE ON TOP OF TWO OVALS TO CREATE THE HEAD AND BASIC BODY SHAPE OF A BUTTERFLY.

2

SKETCH A TOP WING ON EITHER SIDE OF THE BODY. THEN ADD A TEARDROP ON EACH SIDE FOR THE SMALLER WINGS, AS SHOWN.

3

DRAW A SYMMETRICAL PATTERN ON THE WINGS, MIRRORING OVAL AND RECTANGLE SHAPES ON EACH SIDE. ADD TWO LINES FOR THE ANTENNAE.

4

USE MORE SYMMETRY WHEN YOU COLOUR THE BUTTERFLY, MAKING SURE BOTH WINGS ARE A MIRROR IMAGE OF EACH OTHER.

Try drawing different-shaped wings. Start with one side then just repeat on the other!

Vary the patterns, trying circles, ovals and rectangles. Try mixing shapes together for new patterns.

EXPERIMENT WITH MORE ELABORATE PATTERNS...

SPOTTY

Decorate the wings with different-sized spots, circles and stripes.

Use only three colours, but use different shades of each for depth.

Add outlines around some shapes to make them stand out.

SWIRLY

Draw darker, swirly lines inside light pencil wing shapes.

Trace around the swirls in coloured pens. Rub away any pencil marks.

Colour big swirls in one colour and small swirls in another.

STRIPY

Try spots, stripes and teardrops on wavy-edged wings.

Colour the pattern in a mixture of complementary shades and colours.

Draw a thin border around some of the pattern for emphasis.

51

MOUTHS

Drawing a mouth front on

1 SKETCH A RECTANGLE, THEN ADD A VERTICAL AND HORIZONTAL LINE AS SHOWN. USE THESE GUIDES TO DRAW A BASIC MOUTH SHAPE.

2 SKETCH A CURVED MOUTH SHAPE OVER YOUR GUIDELINE. THE TOP LIP IS A BIT LIKE THE LETTER 'M', THE BOTTOM LIKE A WIDE 'U'.

3 ADD SHADING AND COLOUR TO YOUR LIPS. THE SHADING NEEDS TO LOOK SLIGHTLY CURVED TO MAKE THE LIPS LOOK 3D.

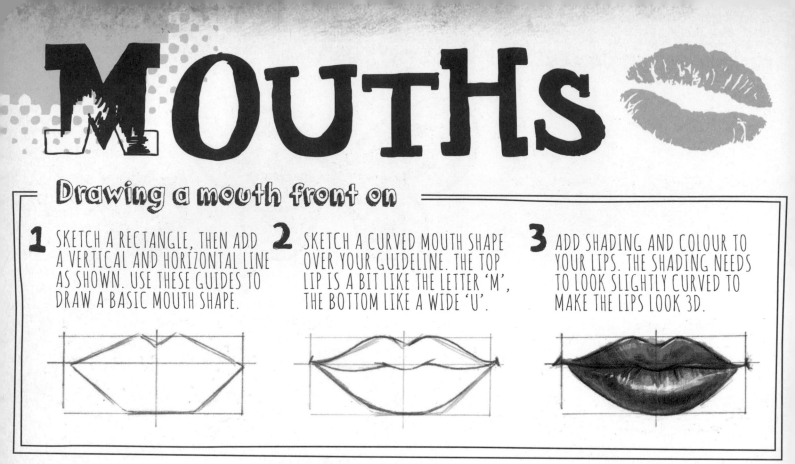

Drawing at an angle

Lips are a surprisingly complex shape, which is more noticeable when you draw them at an angle. The top lip tends to stick out slightly more than the bottom one, while the lower lip curves under smoothly.

When someone's mouth is slightly open, you'll see the full, rounded shape of the lips.

To sketch a mouth that's fully open, make the lips look thinner since they would be stretched tighter across the teeth.

Creating Expressions

HAPPY
The top lip looks like a shallow 'M' shape with turned-up corners. The teeth can be close together or slightly apart.

ANGRY
The teeth and gums are visible and the top lip looks stretched out.

WORRIED OR CONFUSED
Sketch the upper teeth biting part of the lower lip. One corner of the bottom lip should also droop down.

TALKING
The lips are relaxed and the overall mouth shape is squarer. The teeth and tongue are slightly visible.

POUTING
To draw a pout, make the top lip thin, with the lower lip jutting out, full and rounded.

SHOUT
Draw both the top and bottom lips in a stretched position, with the teeth wide apart.

SCREAM
Sketch an 'O'-shaped mouth with the lips stretched very thin. Draw the tongue and tonsils too!

PUCKERED
The lips look as if they've been squashed in from the sides, making both of them full in shape.

BLIMPS

1

SKETCH A STRAIGHT HORIZONTAL LINE. DRAW AN OVAL SHAPE AROUND IT, TAPERING OFF ONE END TO FORM A POINT.

2

ADD THE TAIL FINS AT THE END OF THE BLIMP. DRAW THE PASSENGER CAR BENEATH THE OVAL, AS SHOWN.

3

DRAW ANOTHER TAIL FIN AT AN ANGLE. SKETCH CURVED GUIDELINES ON THE BLIMP, AS SHOWN. ADD DETAIL TO THE CAR.

Use rectangle shapes for windows and circles for wheels.

4

CHOOSE A PATTERN THEME, LIKE TRIANGLES AND DIAMONDS, AND ADD IT TO THE BLIMP AROUND YOUR GUIDELINES.

5

GO OVER YOUR LINEWORK WITH A BLACK PEN. THEN COLOUR THE BLIMP USING WATERCOLOUR PAINT.

Use a red felt-tip pen for the triangles and diamonds to help them stand out from the background.

Choose bright colours for your blimp so people can see it from the ground.

Try different shapes and patterns for your blimp. Experiment until you are happy with your design!

SYDNEY OPERA HOUSE

Find a reference photo of this famous Australian building before you start.

1

BREAK DOWN THE OPERA HOUSE INTO SIMPLE STAGES. FIRST SKETCH OVERLAPPING TRIANGULAR SHAPES FOR THE SAILS OF THE BUILDING.

2

ADD A RECTANGULAR SHAPE BENEATH THE SAILS FOR THE BASE OF THE BUILDING AND A HORIZONTAL LINE FOR THE GROUND.

Add some people at the bottom of the building to give a sense of its huge scale.

3

DRAW LINES INSIDE THE SAILS, AS SHOWN. DARKEN THESE LINES SO THE SHAPE OF THE BUILDING IS CLEAR.

4

START FILLING IN THE DETAIL. DRAW MORE TRIANGULAR SHAPES INSIDE THE SAILS AND ADD RECTANGULAR WINDOWS AND DOORS AT THE BASE OF THE BUILDING.

Use light and medium blues on the white sails for shading. Darken the areas inside the sails and on the windows to suggest the direction of light.

5

USE PEN OR INK TO GO AROUND THE OUTLINE OF THE BUILDING. ADD SOME HATCHING TO THE SAILS. THEN ADD COLOUR! INCLUDE A HINT OF WATER FOR THE SETTING.

GYMNAST

1

DRAW A SIMPLE LINE OF ACTION FOR THE BASIC POSE AND GUIDES FOR THE BARS. GYMNASTS HAVE SUPPLE, BENDY BODIES!

2

ADD CONSTRUCTION SHAPES FOR THE DIFFERENT BODY PARTS, USING CIRCLES, OVALS AND STICK LINES, TO SET YOUR PROPORTIONS.

3

DRAW THE OUTLINE OF THE BODY AROUND YOUR GUIDES. SKETCH SIMPLE SHAPES FOR THE ARMS, HANDS, LEGS AND FEET.

4

REFINE YOUR PENCIL LINES TO DEFINE THE BODY SHAPE. ADD MUSCLE TONE, BODY CONTOURS AND THE SHAPE OF THE HEAD.

Start rubbing out your construction shapes and stick lines as you build up the detail in your drawing.

Add a couple of curved lines that follow the shape of the gymnast's body. These help create an impression of movement.

5

DRAW IN THE FACIAL FEATURES, ADD SHADING TO THE MUSCLES AND GIVE THE CLOTHES SOME CREASES. REFINE THE SET OF PARALLEL BARS TOO.

6

PAINT YOUR DRAWING. USE BOTH LIGHTER AND DARKER TONES FOR THE GYMNAST'S BARE SKIN TO MAKE THOSE MUSCLES POP.

Find a colour wheel to help you choose which colours to use. Here, the warm red and cool blue complement each other well.

Adding a few small lines to the parallel bars helps to make them look 3D.

MOUSTACHES

HAVE FUN DRAWING SIMPLE BUT EFFECTIVE MOUSTACHES. ADD THEM TO YOUR DRAWINGS OF PEOPLE OR CREATE YOUR OWN MUST-HAVE MOUSTACHE FASHION ON T-SHIRTS OR BAGS WITH SOLID BLACK STYLIZED SHAPES.

1

DRAW A VERY WIDE 'M' SHAPE FOR THE BASIC OUTLINE OF A MOUSTACHE, LIKE THIS.

2

SKETCH SOFT CURVED LINES FLOWING OUT FROM THE MIDDLE OF YOUR 'TACHE, FOLLOWING ITS SHAPE. VARY THE PRESSURE OF YOUR PENCIL FOR INDIVIDUAL STRANDS.

3

NOW PAINT YOUR MOUSTACHE! USE LIGHT SHADING IN THE CENTRE, GRADUALLY GOING DARKER TOWARDS THE ENDS. ADD SHADING BETWEEN THE LINES.

NOW TRY DIFFERENT STYLES:

UPSIDE-DOWN

HAIR FLICKS

CURLY ENDS

MINI 'TACHE

NOW TRY THESE FUNNY STYLES, USING A BLACK MARKER OR PEN.

Bold 'm' shape with long, curved sides and frayed ends.

Wide 'm' shape, with a narrow middle and upward curving sides.

Thick and chunky 'm' shape, with swirly, twirly ends.

Thick, semi-circular 'm' shape with downward, pointy ends.

Small, wavy 'm' shape, like an upside-down tulip.

Angular 'm' shape, like an inverted horseshoe.

Tall and chunky 'm' shape with spindly curls at the ends.

Squashed 'm' shape with thick, curly ends.

Thick and curvy 'm' shape with soft, curly ends.

Split-down-the-middle 'm' shape, with spiky ends.

Wide, angular 'm' shape with pointy, tapered ends.

Wide, straight-edged 'm' shape, with curved, pointy ends.

WIZARD

As you add more detail, rub out any guidelines you don't need to stop your drawing looking messy!

1
DRAW SIMPLE OUTLINES FOR THE BODY SHAPE, AS SHOWN. ADD A SWEEPING CURVE FOR HIS CLOAK, PLUS A HAT AND SCEPTRE GUIDE.

2
FLESH OUT THE ARMS, HANDS, CLOAK AND SLEEVES. USE A BOX SHAPE FOR THE SPELL BOOK AND CURVES FOR THE CHEST STRAP.

3
DRAW GUIDELINES ON THE FACE, THEN SKETCH THE WIZARD'S FEATURES. ADD FINGER DETAILS AND CREASES TO THE HAT AND TROUSERS. DRAW SQUARES AND CIRCLES FOR THE JEWELLERY.

If you're not sure how to draw something in detail, it's a good idea to sketch simple guidelines and rough shapes first to help you!

4

CONCENTRATE ON THE FINE DETAILS, DRAWING SQUARES AND ZIG-ZAG PATTERNS ON THE WIZARD'S CLOTHES. ADD MORE LINES TO THE BOOK AND DRAW AN EXTRA OVAL SHAPE UNDER THE HAT BRIM.

Paint lots of swirling, colourful flame-like shapes to create magic!

5

GIVE YOUR WIZARD COLOURFUL CLOTHES AND JEWELLERY. EARTHY TONES SUCH AS GREENS, BROWNS AND DARK ORANGES WORK WELL. ADD SHADOWS AND HIGHLIGHTS TO GIVE YOUR FIGURE SOME DEPTH.

BULLDOG IN A BOW TIE

1 DRAW CIRCLES FOR THE DOG'S HEAD, BODY AND OUTSIDE LEG, A SEMI-CIRCLE FOR THE INSIDE LEG AND LINES FOR THE LEGS AND FEET.

2 SKETCH AN OUTLINE AROUND THE SHAPES TO JOIN THEM TOGETHER. DRAW A CROSS ON THE FACE AS A GUIDE FOR THE BULLDOG'S FEATURES AND ADD TRIANGULAR SHAPES FOR THE EARS AND TAIL.

Look at pictures of bulldogs online or in books for reference as you draw.

3 SKETCH CIRCLES FOR THE EYES, AN OVAL FOR THE NOSE, A WIDE 'W' SHAPE FOR THE MOUTH AND CURVED LINES FOR THE TONGUE AND CHIN. DRAW A RECTANGLE AND TRIANGULAR SHAPES FOR THE BOW TIE, AS SHOWN.

4 USE A STRONGER OUTLINE TO GO AROUND THE BULLDOG SHAPE, ADDING IN MORE DETAIL LIKE CURVED LINES FOR WRINKLES AND PAWS. RUB AWAY ANY LINES YOU NO LONGER NEED.

5 PRESS HARDER ON THE PENCIL TO START SHADING IN SOME OF THE DETAIL AROUND ONE EYE, THE NOSE, MOUTH AND PAWS. DRAW DIAGONAL LINES ON THE BOW TIE AND ADD CURVED LINES FOR CREASES.

6 COLOUR THE DOG IN DIFFERENT TONES OF BROWN, WHITE AND GREY. ADD SHORT, SHARP PENCIL STROKES TO SUGGEST FUR. LEAVE GLINTS IN THIS CHEEKY DOG'S EYES!

Use smooth pencil strokes to colour the bow tie. Add highlighted areas to suggest a silky shine and realistic folds.

BOW TIES!

Try different patterns on your bow tie. Experiment with various shapes and colours. Tie-tastic!

PAISLEY PATTERN

1
FIRST DRAW ONE PIECE: SKETCH A CIRCLE WITH A BEAK SHAPE ON TOP TO FORM AN ANGLED TEARDROP.

2
DRAW ANOTHER TEARDROP INSIDE IT, FOLLOWING THE SAME SHAPE AS THE ONE ON THE OUTSIDE.

3
SKETCH A BRANCH AND LEAF PATTERN DESIGN INSIDE THE SMALLER TEARDROP.

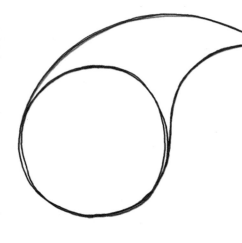

4
ADD MORE DETAIL, LIKE A WAVY OUTLINE, SHORT FINE LINES ON THE LEAVES, SMALL DOTS AND OVERLAPPING CIRCLES, AS SHOWN.

5
SKETCH SEMI-CIRCLES IN THE BORDER BETWEEN THE TEARDROPS AND A WAVY SHAPE OVER THE TOP OF THE INNER TEARDROP.

6
DRAW OVER THE OUTLINES WITH A FINE PEN AND RUB AWAY THE PENCIL LINES. NOW HAVE FUN COLOURING YOUR DESIGN!

CREATE MORE TEARDROP SHAPES, LIKE THE ONES BELOW, EXPERIMENTING WITH DIFFERENT DESIGNS INSIDE. THEN PUT THEM TOGETHER TO MAKE THE PAISLEY PATTERN!

Paisley is a pretty, swirly Indian pattern often used on shawls, scarves or ties. It's right on trend!

Add flowers and stars to your paisley designs - the more elaborate, the better!

Pair a warm colour, like yellow, with cool colours, such as blue and green, for perfect paisley harmony!

WEIGHTLIFTER

1

USING A LIGHT 2H PENCIL, SKETCH A STICK MAN TO SET YOUR BASIC WEIGHTLIFTING POSE. MAKE THE KNEES SLIGHTLY BENT.

2

DRAW THE WEIGHTLIFTER'S OUTLINE AROUND YOUR GUIDE. MAKE HIS MUSCULAR LEGS AND BICEPS EXTRA CHUNKY.

3

SKETCH CURVED LINES TO DEFINE THE MUSCLE TONE. OUTLINE THE CLOTHING, ROUGH FACIAL FEATURES AND THE BARBELLS.

Find a photo of a weightlifter to help you work out how big the different sets of muscles should look.

A weightlifter's clothing is usually very tight, so you only really need to sketch in the outlines of his vest and shorts.

Add white bands to the barbell weights to give the impression of a shiny, reflective surface.

4

WORK OUT WHERE THE LIGHT SOURCE IS AND USE A HEAVIER 4B PENCIL TO ADD THE SHADOWY AREAS. THESE WILL HELP TO PICK OUT THE SHAPES OF THE MUSCLES.

5

GO OVER YOUR LINEWORK AND SHADOWED AREAS IN BLACK INK. PAINT YOUR FIGURE'S SKIN IN DIFFERENT TONES, THEN GIVE HIM A BOLD-COLOURED OUTFIT TO WEAR.

Make some of the muscle areas completely black to make your character look really strong and powerful!

TREES

BASIC TREE

Draw a rough bushy outline, then add a few branches, varying the thickness of each one. Draw simple leaf shapes in the gaps.

Use black ink to draw a bare tree that looks like it's been scorched!

PINE TREE

Sketch the trunk first, then add branches on both sides, each one angled slightly upwards. Next, add lots of needles using short, thin lines.

For a natural look, give your tree drawings quirks and irregularities. For example, some branches or twigs could look bare, apart from a couple of leaves!

Notice how some pine branches can divide up into more smaller branches.

CHERRY TREE IN BLOSSOM

Draw a short tree trunk breaking into branches. Use ink for the blossom shapes then add a blob of pink paint to each one.

Practise drawing the blossom in detail. You may want to simplify it a bit, depending on the size of your drawing.

HOLLY TREE

Draw a rough triangle for the basic tree shape, then add clusters of round berries, each surrounded by a group of leaves.

When you draw holly close up, use small, curved lines to sketch each pointed leaf shape.

LEAVES

Draw the central vein, then add the pointed oval shape. Fill the space with smaller veins.

For this leaf, draw the main vein and smaller veins, then sketch the wobbly leaf outline.

Start with five finger lines, then add the jagged shape of the leaf around them.

Draw a curved line, thicker at one end than the other. Add horizontal curves and then sketch small leaves.

BIG BEN

4

DRAW THE INTRICATE CLOCK FACE AND ADD MORE SURFACE DETAIL ON EITHER SIDE. USE A DARK PENCIL TO ADD SHADING TO THE INDENTED SHAPES ON THE TOWER'S SURFACE.

Big Ben is one of the most famous London landmarks, so it'll be easy to find a good reference photo online.

1

DRAW THE BASIC OUTLINE OF BIG BEN USING SQUARES, RECTANGLES AND TRIANGULAR SHAPES. DIVIDE THE TOWER BENEATH THE CLOCK INTO FOUR EQUAL-SIZED SECTIONS.

Draw 12 guidelines to help you position each number in the right place on the clock face.

5

PAINT YOUR PICTURE A LIGHT SHADE OF BROWN, ADDING DARKER PATCHES TO SUGGEST AREAS THAT ARE IN SHADOW. PICK OUT DETAILS AROUND THE CLOCK FACE IN YELLOW.

2

DRAW MORE HORIZONTAL LINES TO BUILD UP THE SURFACE DETAIL A LITTLE. SKETCH TWO SQUARE SHAPES TO MAKE A FRAME FOR THE CLOCK FACE.

3

DRAW SEVEN TALL SHAPES ON EACH OF THE SQUARE SECTIONS. GIVE EACH ONE A POINTED TIP. ADD EXTRA ARCHES AND WINDOWS NEAR THE TOP OF THE TOWER.

LOCH NESS MONSTER

NO ONE KNOWS IF THIS FAMOUS CREATURE FROM SCOTLAND REALLY EXISTS. BUT YOU CAN CREATE A VERY REAL DRAWING OF IT!

1 SKETCH A ROUGH OVAL SHAPE FOR THE MONSTER'S BODY AND A LONG ROUNDED CYLINDER SHAPE FOR THE NECK, AS SHOWN.

2 DRAW SQUASHED OVAL SHAPES FOR THE HEAD, TAIL AND ONE OF THE BACK FINS. DRAW TWO SMALL OVALS UNDER THE BODY.

Sketch the tail and large fin at an angle for a swimming creature.

3 ADD A CIRCULAR EYE, A CURVED LINE FOR THE MOUTH AND A WING-SHAPED FIN ON THE BODY. START DRAWING AN OUTLINE AROUND THE SHAPES TO LINK THEM ALL TOGETHER.

4

GO OVER YOUR OUTLINE WITH AN INK PEN, THEN
RUB AWAY THE PENCIL MARKS. DRAW SPOTS AND
CREASES IN THE SKIN, AND A PUPIL FOR THE EYE.

Draw a straight line for the
water level. Add some hilly land
in the distance, and wavy lines in
front for a rippling water effect.

Make the areas on the
monster's underside darker
to show that the light is
coming from above the water.

5

FINISH YOUR CREATURE WITH WATERCOLOUR PAINTS. ADD
LOTS OF COLOUR FOR THE DARK AREAS AND MIX IN MORE
WATER FOR LIGHTER COLOURS. GIVE YOUR MONSTER A 3D
EFFECT WITH THESE VARIED SHADES AND BRING IT TO LIFE!

MAGNIFYING GLASS

WHEN YOU DRAW AS IF THROUGH A MAGNIFYING GLASS, YOU CAN ADD FANTASTIC-LOOKING DETAILS YOU MIGHT NOT OTHERWISE SEE!

1 BEFORE YOU START DRAWING, FIND A PHOTO OF YOUR IMAGE ONLINE OR CHOOSE ONE FROM A BOOK. THIS WILL HELP YOU GET THE TINY DETAILS RIGHT.

2 USING A PENCIL, DRAW A BIG CIRCLE FOR THE MAGNIFYING GLASS, THEN BUILD UP THE HANDLE SHAPE WITH DIFFERENT-SIZED RECTANGES. SKETCH SIMPLE SHAPES TO FORM A BUTTERFLY'S BODY.

3 START ADDING MORE DETAIL TO THE DIFFERENT BODY PARTS. DRAW EXTRA LINES ON THE WINGS AND A FEW MORE CURVES ON THE HEAD SECTION.

4 CONCENTRATE ON THE FINE DETAILS USING A SHARP PENCIL. DRAW TINY HAIRS ON THE BUTTERFLY'S HEAD AND LEGS, THEN ADD PATTERNS OF SHADING TO ITS WINGS.

5

USE AN INK PEN TO GO OVER THE PENCIL LINES AND SHADED AREAS. COLOUR YOUR BUTTERFLY USING INKS IN DIFFERENT TONES AND LEAVE TO DRY. FINALLY, USE COLOURED PENCILS TO ADD SOME SUBTLE SHADED TEXTURE ON TOP.

Think about how the bits enlarged through the magnifying glass will look different to the smaller version outside the glass.

To create reflections on the glass, add bands of watery white paint over the top of your butterfly.

1

START BY SKETCHING THE CAR AT AN ANGLE, WITH THREE OVALS FOR THE WHEELS. USE CURVED LINES FOR THE MAIN SHAPE. ADD A STRAIGHT LINE NEAR THE TOP.

2

USE VERTICAL LINES FOR THE WINDSCREEN AND WINDOWS. THEN ADD WAVY LINES TO CREATE THE CAR'S BASIC BODY CURVES.

3

DRAW THE TYRES, RIMS, HEADLIGHTS, WING MIRRORS AND BUMPER USING A MIXTURE OF LINES, RECTANGLES, TRIANGLES AND CIRCLES, AS SHOWN.

4

GO OVER YOUR DRAWING WITH A SOFT
LEADED PENCIL. LIGHTLY SHADE THE BODY
TO HIGHLIGHT THE CURVES. ADD DARK
SHADING ON THE WHEELS.

5 FINISH WITH A BRIGHT COLOUR FOR THE BODY.
REMEMBER TO GRADUALLY BUILD UP YOUR
SHADING FOR A REALISTIC EFFECT, GOING WITH
THE CONTOURS OF THE CAR FOR A SLEEK LOOK.

Add lots of white to the windscreen
for a really bright reflection.

Add shiny highlights on the car, using small amounts of white colour.
Apply sparingly to keep your drawing looking realistic.

CAT IN SUNGLASSES

LEARN TO DRAW A PICTURE OF A CAT, THEN GIVE IT SOME PERSONALITY WITH A PAIR OF COOL-LOOKING SHADES. PURR-FECT!

1 SKETCH THREE CIRCLE GUIDES FOR THE CAT'S BODY. ADD EARS AND A TAIL. USE A RULER TO ADD A HORIZONAL LINE IN THE BACKGROUND.

2 DRAW TWO CIRCLES TO PLACE THE CAT'S BACK PAWS. DRAW TWO STRAIGHT LEGS AT THE FRONT TO SHOW THE CAT SITTING UP.

3 ADD TWO DOTS FOR THE CAT'S EYES, A SMALL TRIANGLE FOR HER NOSE AND AN UPSIDE-DOWN 'Y' FOR THE MOUTH.

Sketch curved lines on the body to give the idea of a thick, fluffy coat.

4 APPLY SHORT WIGGLY LINES OVER YOUR PENCIL MARKS TO SUGGEST FUR. THEN ADD A POINTY CURVE BENEATH THE CAT'S MOUTH FOR A CHIN.

Draw six sloping lines for the cat's whiskers.

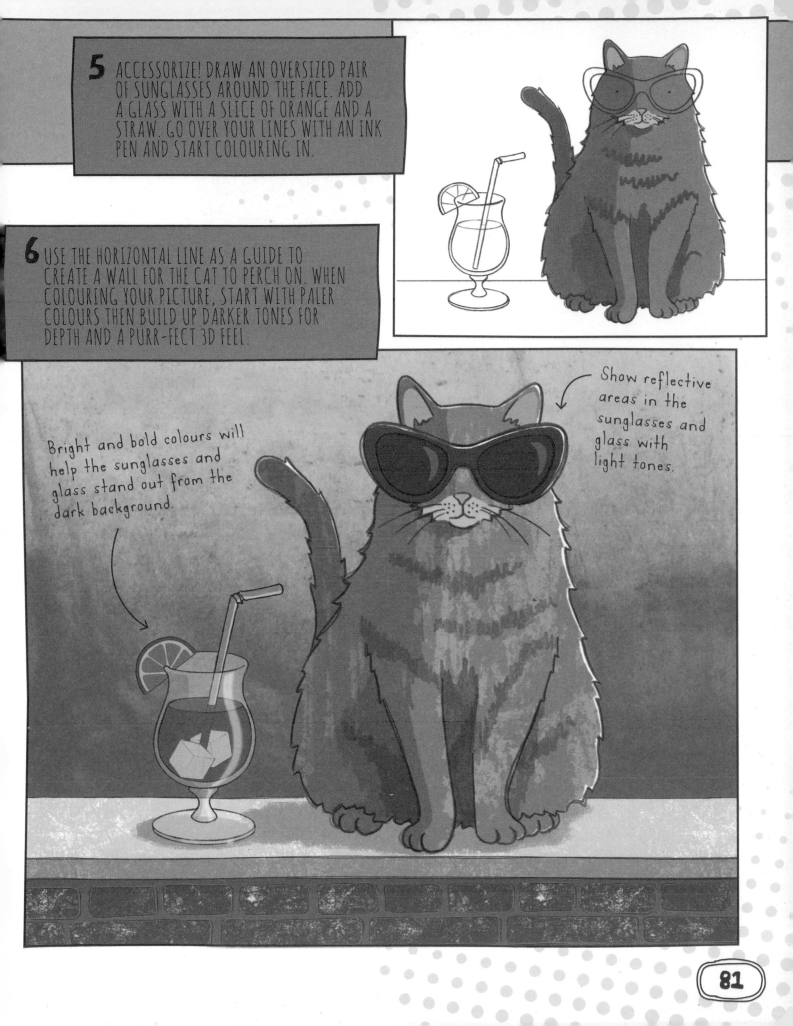

5 ACCESSORIZE! DRAW AN OVERSIZED PAIR OF SUNGLASSES AROUND THE FACE. ADD A GLASS WITH A SLICE OF ORANGE AND A STRAW. GO OVER YOUR LINES WITH AN INK PEN AND START COLOURING IN.

6 USE THE HORIZONTAL LINE AS A GUIDE TO CREATE A WALL FOR THE CAT TO PERCH ON. WHEN COLOURING YOUR PICTURE, START WITH PALER COLOURS THEN BUILD UP DARKER TONES FOR DEPTH AND A PURR-FECT 3D FEEL.

Show reflective areas in the sunglasses and glass with light tones.

Bright and bold colours will help the sunglasses and glass stand out from the dark background.

Find a photo of the White House for inspiration before you start drawing.

1

USE A RULER TO DRAW A HORIZONTAL RECTANGULAR SHAPE, LIKE THIS. DRAW A GUIDELINE DOWN THE CENTRE.

2

SKETCH A RECTANGLE AROUND THE GUIDELINE AND A TRIANGLE AT THE TOP. ADD A HORIZONTAL LINE UNDER THE TOP OF YOUR LARGE RECTANGLE.

3

DRAW AN UPSIDE-DOWN TRAPEZOID SHAPE BENEATH THE TRIANGLE. ADD FOUR MORE HORIZONTAL LINES FOR WINDOW GUIDES. THE TOP TWO LINES SHOULD BE CLOSER TOGETHER AS THESE WINDOWS ARE SHORTER. ADD TWO SMALL RECTANGULAR CHIMNEYS AND A CIRCLE AT THE TOP OF THE FLAG POLE.

4

DRAW RECTANGLES, TRIANGLES, CYLINDERS, CIRCLES AND OVALS FOR THE WINDOWS, DOOR, ROOF, COLUMNS AND HANGING LIGHT, AS SHOWN. RUB AWAY ANY GUIDELINES.

Use wavy lines to create the effect of bushes and a flag.

Sketch oval-shaped posts for the balustrade.

5

ADD DETAILS TO THE WINDOWS, ROOF, FOUNTAIN AND BUSHES USING CRISS-CROSS LINES, SEMI-CIRCLES, TRIANGLES, OVALS AND CURVED LINES, LIKE THIS.

6 NOW COLOUR YOUR PICTURE, USING LONG, SWEEPING STROKES FOR THE BUILDING AND SHORT, DABBING STROKES FOR THE RED FLOWERS AND GREEN BUSHES.

Follow the flag's wavy outline when you paint for a rippling effect.

Paint bluey-grey shades on the building and windows to show reflections from the sky.

TREE BARK

These tree pictures were created using 'mixed media', which means you can combine different materials to get the right texture or effect! Pen, pencil, ink and gouache (a thick kind of paint) all work well together.

Create this bark by using a pencil to shade long, vertical strips. Then use an ink pen to add some crosshatch areas on top.

Using different shades of green, dab the end of your paintbrush onto the paper to get this leafy effect,

Use a soft pencil and flow the pencil marks in different directions to produce a natural-looking texture.

Old trees are all gnarled and knotty, which makes them really interesting to draw! Sketch the shape of the tree first, using long wavy lines to form the roots, trunk and branches.

Draw oval and spiral shapes for the knots. Add tones of pencil shading, and pen lines for extra texture.

Silver birches are beautiful trees to draw, with their long trunks, slender branches and distinct bark. Draw the outlines of the trees before adding detail.

Draw lots of horizontal pencil marks for the bark texture. Then add random patches of light and dark shading.

85

3D MAZE

1

START WITH A FLAT MAZE TO MAP OUT YOUR ROUTE. DRAW A BIG RECTANGLE, THEN USE A RULER TO DRAW DOUBLED LINES FOR THE MAZE INSIDE. MAKE SURE THERE IS ONLY ONE WAY THROUGH. USE SHORT LINES FOR DEAD ENDS.

2

NOW DRAW YOUR MAZE IN 3D! ANGLE THE RECTANGLE BACK WITH THE SIDES SLANTING INWARDS. THEN DRAW THE LINES INSIDE IT, COPYING THE ROUTE YOU SET IN YOUR FLAT MAZE.

IN

3 USE TRACING PAPER TO COPY AND PRINT YOUR MAZE OVER THE ORIGINAL, BUT MOVE IT SLIGHTLY LOWER DOWN, AS SHOWN.

This isn't any ordinary maze! Add extra details like pipes, aerials and steam for personality. Don't forget the person about to get lost in there!

4

DRAW VERTICAL AND HORIZONTAL LINES TO LINK UP THE MATCHING BITS OF THE MAZES AND CREATE A 3D SHAPE, AS SHOWN.

5

ADD SHADING TO ALL THE SIDE WALLS, AND MAKE THE FRONT WALLS LIGHTER TO SUGGEST THE DIRECTION OF LIGHT. THEN COLOUR YOUR MAZE!

OUT

SUNRISE

1 SKETCH A ROUGH LANDSCAPE USING SIMPLE CURVES. DRAW TRIANGULAR SHAPES FOR TREES.

2 KEEPING YOUR LINEWORK LOOSE, SKETCH A RISING SUN IN THE DISTANCE. ADD OTHER DETAILS SUCH AS A HOUSE AND ROWING BOAT. SKETCH IN MORE LANDSCAPE FEATURES AS WELL.

Use lighter shades for the middle area of your picture. This will help draw your eye to the most interesting parts - the sun, house and rowing boat.

Think about how the sunlight affects the objects in your picture. Draw some birds silhouetted against the dazzling sky and add highlights to the rippling water. The hills just below are lit by the sun too.

3 REFINE THE OUTLINES OF THE DIFFERENT SHAPES AND USE A RULER TO DRAW LONG SUNBEAMS RADIATING OUT FROM THE SUN. NOW START TO BLOCK IN ROUGH AREAS OF COLOUR.

4 USE DIFFERENT SHADES OF YOUR CHOSEN COLOURS TO ADD DEPTH AND DETAIL. FADE BETWEEN THE YELLOWS AND ORANGES OF THE SUNRISE AND THE PURPLY TONES OF THE SKY. A SUNRISE IS ALL ABOUT THE COLOUR AND FEEL!

SHOES

DRAW DIFFERENT STYLES OF FOOTWEAR, THEN CREATE YOUR OWN PATTERNED FASHIONS!

1

USE CURVED LINES TO DRAW THE SIMPLE SHAPE OF A TRAINER.

2

ADD IN THE RUBBER SOLE, THE TONGUE, LACES AND EDGING, AS SHOWN.

3

DRAW LINES TO SUGGEST DIFFERENT FABRICS ON THE SIDES AND AROUND THE BACK. SKETCH DASHED LINES FOR STITCHING, AND ADD A PATTERN.

ONCE YOU'VE MASTERED THE BASIC SHOE, TRY THESE TECHNIQUES...

BROGUE SHOE

Vary the shape of your shoe and include brogue-type stitching using circles and zig zags.

Draw shapes on your shoe to suggest multiple fabrics.

Create laces from short and long lines, and ovals.

This zig-zag pattern uses small teeth-like lines to frame the fabric.

PLATFORM

Exaggerate the shoe's arch, heel and sole to create a high-heeled platform shoe.

This zig-zag pattern uses bold, contrasting colours for the overall pattern of the shoe.

TRY BUILDING UP SIMPLE SHAPES TO CREATE COOL SHOE PATTERNS.

THE CHEQUERED PUMP

Horizontal and vertical lines create an eye-catching two-tone chequered pattern.

Contrasting and complementary colours help make patterns like stars, spots and zig-zags pop.

THE STARRY HIGH TOP

Isolate your pattern to just one part of the shoe for a pattern pop!

THE BALLET PUMP

Sketch a long oval shape, then draw curved lines around it to create a ballet shoe.

Repeat semi-circles for a rainbow pattern.

Break up a spotty pattern with a chunky rectangular band.

THE KITTEN HEEL

Draw a simple shoe shape and add a small heel.

Use curved shapes, spiralling outwards from the centre, for a rose pattern.

Curvy rectangles make this simple shoe buckle for a higher-heeled shoe.

ROBOT

1 DRAW STICK LINES FOR THE GENERAL SHAPE AND LIMBS. MAKE THE ARMS LONG TO GIVE A SENSE OF THE ROBOT LEANING FORWARDS.

2 USE SIMPLE OVALS TO FLESH OUT THE SHAPES OF THE HEAD, CHEST AND HIP AREA. ADD SIMPLE LINES FOR THE HANDS.

3 DRAW MORE OVALS FOR THE SHOULDERS, ARMS AND LEGS. USE SEMI-CIRCLES AND RECTANGLES TO SKETCH FEET.

4 FLESH OUT YOUR STICK FIGURE EVEN MORE. JOIN THE OVALS WITH THICKER LINES, ADD TUBING BEHIND THE HEAD AND DRAW FINGERS ON EACH HAND.

5 START ADDING LINES AND CURVES TO THE BODY PARTS TO MAKE THEM LOOK MORE 3D. DRAW IN THE ROBOT'S FACIAL FEATURES AND ADD MORE SURFACE DETAIL.

6 CONCENTRATE ON THE FINER DETAILS, ADDING THINGS LIKE WIRES AND RIVETS. DRAW LOTS OF TINY LINES TO GIVE CERTAIN AREAS A TUBE-LIKE TEXTURE.

7 PAINT YOUR ROBOT IN DIFFERENT SHADES OF GREY. USE A SINGLE BASE COLOUR TO START WITH, THEN ADD LIGHTER GREYS FOR THE HIGHLIGHTED AREAS WITH DARKER TONES FOR THE AREAS THAT ARE IN SHADE.

Pick out some of the smaller details in bright colours. These will help add interest to your drawing.

Painting bands of lighter and darker greys will help give the robot's body a more metallic and reflective texture.

Use a watery grey wash for the robot's reflections. These help connect the robot to its background.

93

VINTAGE BICYCLE

1 BREAK THE BICYCLE INTO SIMPLE SHAPES. DRAW TWO CIRCLES FOR THE WHEELS, THEN USE A RULER TO JOIN THEM TOGETHER. DRAW TWO ANGLED LINES FOR THE FRAME AND A SHORT LINE FOR THE SEAT.

2 USE RECTANGLES, STRAIGHT LINES AND CURVED LINES TO ADD MORE DETAIL TO THE FRAMEWORK, AND TO CREATE HANDLEBARS AND A SHOPPING BASKET, AS SHOWN.

3 SKETCH A RECTANGLE FOR THE SEAT AND A SPIRAL FOR ITS SPRING. DRAW MORE CIRCLES FOR THE WHEELS, CHAIN WHEEL AND HUB. ADD A CYLINDER-SHAPED CHAIN AND A TRIANGULAR HEADLIGHT.

4 FOR THE SPOKES, DRAW LINES RADIATING OUT FROM THE WHEEL HUB AND CHAIN. THEN START TO GO OVER YOUR LINES WITH A WATER-RESISTANT INK PEN. RUB AWAY ANY PENCIL MARKS.

5 USING THE PEN, DRAW LINES ON THE HANDLEBARS AND THE BASKET TO CREATE TEXTURE. FILL IN THE WHEELS TO MAKE TYRES. ADD A CIRCLE AND LINES ON THE CHAIN WHEEL. DRAW CURVED LINES AROUND THE WHEELS FOR THE MUDGUARDS.

The texture on the basket and handlebars contrasts with the smooth appearance of the frames and spokes.

6 DRAW HANDBRAKES AND PEDALS, AND A LONG CURVED LINE FOR THE BRAKE CABLE. ADD COLOUR USING WATERCOLOUR INK OR PAINTS.

For motion, shade around the spokes with a pencil. Erase some of the pencil marks using a circular movement.

TENNIS PLAYER

1

LIGHTLY SKETCH A STICK FIGURE IN AN ACTION POSE WITH THE LEFT ARM ACROSS THE CHEST, HOLDING ONTO A STICK. THE RIGHT LEG SHOULD BE STRAIGHT AND THE LEFT ONE BENT.

2

SKETCH THE LOOSE OUTLINE OF THE PLAYER AROUND THE GUIDES. THE RIGHT SHOULDER IS SLIGHTLY HIGHER SO THE CLOTHES SHOULD APPEAR SLIGHTLY TWISTED.

3

START WORKING ON THE DETAIL. ADD THE FACIAL FEATURES AND GIVE THE RACQUET SOME SHAPE. USE LIGHT SHADING TO SHOW THE FOLDS IN THE CLOTHES.

Think about which direction
the light is coming from to
help you work out where the
shadowed areas should be.

Add small colourful details for
interest, such as a simple three-
tone design on the racket frame.

5

DRAW A LARGE TENNIS BALL
IN MID-AIR. GO OVER YOUR
DRAWING WITH AN INK PEN,
MAKING THE SHADOWY AREAS
TOTALLY BLACK. FINALLY,
CHOOSE A SPORTY COLOUR
SCHEME FOR THE RACQUET AND
CLOTHING AND FINISH!

4

USING A 4B PENCIL, ADD DEFINED
AREAS OF SHADOW AND MUSCLE TONE.
USE CRISS-CROSSING LINES FOR THE
RACQUET STRINGS AND ADD DETAIL TO
THE HANDS, HAIR AND SHOES.

UNICORN

1

DRAW A STICK FIGURE SHOWING THE UNICORN IN AN ACTION POSE. WORK ON GETTING THE PROPORTIONS RIGHT. ADD A LONG, WAVY LINE FROM THE HEAD DOWN TO THE TIP OF THE TAIL.

2

FLESH OUT THE UNICORN'S HEAD, BODY AND LIMBS. DRAW SMALL CIRCLES FOR THE LEG AND ANKLE JOINTS. USE WAVY LINES FOR THE MANE AND TAIL. ADD A SMALL TRIANGLE FOR A HORN.

3

REFINE THE OUTLINE OF THE UNICORN. RUB OUT THE GUIDELINES. ADD FACIAL FEATURES AND DEFINE THE MANE.

4

GO OVER YOUR DRAWING WITH AN INK PEN, ADDING EXTRA LINES FOR DEFINITION. ADD LOTS OF WAVY LINES TO THE MANE AND TAIL FOR A HAIR TEXTURE. ADD A LITTLE SHADING TO THE HORN TOO.

Use watery white paint to create some magical sparkles! Add lots of dots with the end of a small brush, and paint some swirly lines around the horn too.

Lightly sketch in a fantasy background for context and paint with pretty pale watercolour washes.

Add some white highlights to make the unicorn's mane and tail look shiny and magical.

5

PAINT YOUR UNICORN WHITE, USING BLUEY-GREY TONES FOR AREAS THAT ARE IN SHADOW. MAKE THE MANE AND TAIL YELLOW TO CONTRAST WITH THE WHITE.

AVATAR

AN AVATAR IS A COMPUTER-GENERATED VERSION OF YOU! DRAW YOUR OWN DIGITAL ALTER EGO, MIXING AND MATCHING THESE BODY PARTS.

1 CHOOSE THE FACE SHAPE AND SKIN TONE THAT BEST REPRESENTS YOU. LOOK IN A MIRROR IF YOU'RE NOT SURE!

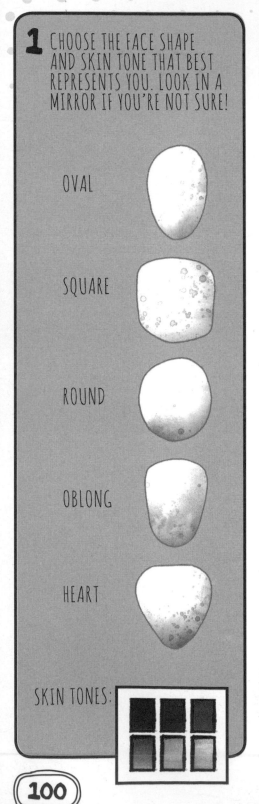

OVAL

SQUARE

ROUND

OBLONG

HEART

SKIN TONES:

2 NOW ADD YOUR HAIRSTYLE. USE LONG, SHORT OR WAVY PENCIL FLICKS AND VARIED COLOUR TONES.

3 EYES AREN'T ALWAYS CIRCULAR. TRY DIFFERENT SHAPES FOR DIFFERENT EXPRESSIONS. SLEEPY, PRETTY OR STARTLED PERHAPS?

IS YOUR AVATAR BRAINY, COOL, BOTH OR NEITHER? IF YOU WANT, DRAW GLASSES OR SHADES TO SUIT YOUR CHARACTER'S PERSONALITY.

4 FOR A BIG NOSE, DRAW LONG LINES AND WIDER CURVES. USE SHORTER, SOFTER LINES FOR A DAINTIER NOSE.

5 YOUR MOUTH COULD BE CHATTY, SHOUTY, SWEET, SHY, TOOTHY OR JUST PLAIN SILLY. IT'S UP TO YOU!

6 SKETCH YOUR BODY SHAPE AND CLOTHES. WILL YOUR AVATAR HAVE A SHORT AND WIDE SUITED-AND-BOOTED BODY, OR A TALL AND THIN DRESSSED-TO-IMPRESS SHAPE? THINK OF A FAVOURITE OUTFIT YOU COULD USE TO REPRESENT YOU.

7 PUT ALL THE BODY PARTS TOGETHER. ADD SOME EYEBROWS AND SEE HOW YOUR AVATAR LOOKS!

GLASSES

FIND OUT HOW TO DRAW DIFFERENT TYPES OF GLASSES. THEN CREATE YOUR OWN FUN STYLES!

1 FOR BASIC FRAMES, DRAW TWO LENS SHAPES. SKETCH A LINE AROUND EACH ONE FOR THE FRAMES AND ADD A BRIDGE WHERE THE GLASSES SIT ON THE NOSE. SHOW THE ARMS THROUGH THE LENSES.

2 COLOUR THE FRAMES, THEN USE A WHITE PENCIL FOR LIGHT DIAGONAL SHADING ON THE LENSES. ADD REFLECTIONS ON EACH ONE, FOLLOWING THE CURVE OF THE FRAMES FOR A 3D EFFECT.

PUT THEM ON!

Draw a character then add in the glasses at an angle to match the face. Lightly shade the lenses so that the character's eyes and face are partially visible beneath.

Colour the frames in similar shades to the clothes and accessories worn by your character. Super stylish! Use dark lenses for sunglasses.

NOW EXPERIMENT WITH MORE COLOURS, PATTERNS AND SHAPES...

BLOCK COLOUR

DRAW SIMPLE LENS SHAPES, THEN FRAME THEM IN BRIGHT AND BOLD COLOURS FOR STATEMENT STYLE.

HALF-MOON

ROUND

PERFECT PATTERNS

CREATE A GINGHAM PRINT WITH CRISS-CROSSING LINES OR TRY A WACKY ANIMAL PRINT MADE WITH SPOTS AND NATURAL COLOURS.

MOVIE STAR

POP STAR

FUN SHAPES

SKETCH YOUR OWN FUN-SHAPED FRAMES. THEN USE CONTRASTING OR COMPLEMENTARY COLOURS ON THE LENSES FOR STYLIN' SHADES.

HEART

STARRY

FASHION SHADES

FOR A TRENDY PAIR OF SUNGLASSES, COLOUR THE LENSES IN A DARK SHADE. KEEP THE ARMS JUST VISIBLE BENEATH.

AVIATOR

DESIGNER

WINDMILL

1 START WITH A BASIC CONE WITH A ROUNDED-OFF TIP. USE A PENCIL AT THIS STAGE.

2 DRAW FOUR TRIANGULAR SHAPES TO MAKE THE SAILS. TRY TO DRAW THEM AS IF YOU'RE LOOKING AT THE WINDMILL FROM THE SIDE. THEN SKETCH THE UPPER SECTION OF THE BUILDING.

Drawing the sails from a side-on perspective will help add movement to your drawing. The ones that are furthest away from us need to look a little smaller.

3 ADD STRAIGHT LINES TO THE SIDES OF THE WINDMILL AND TO THE SAILS.

4 DRAW A BASE WITH CURVED SIDES AND RAILINGS TO ANCHOR THE BUILDING TO THE GROUND.

5 DRAW WINDOWS ON THE SIDES OF THE WINDMILL. ADD A COUPLE FROM A SIDE-ON PERSPECTIVE TO MAKE THE DRAWING LOOK 3D. ADD A RECTANGLE FOR THE FRONT DOOR.

Don't worry if your sails look a bit uneven. This will make your windmill look man-made! Paint them in brown tones to suggest they're made of wood.

Paint one side a slightly lighter shade. This gives the impression of light reflecting off the windmill.

6 USING A WATERPROOF INK PEN, TRACE OVER YOUR DRAWING. ADD WINDOW AND DOOR DETAILS, THEN ADD LOTS OF HORIZONTAL LINES TO SUGGEST THE BUILDING IS MADE OF WOODEN PLANKS. FINALLY, ADD COLOUR USING WATERCOLOUR INKS OR PAINTS.

EXPRESSIONS

HAPPY

Draw the mouth with upturned corners. Make each eyelid cover the iris just a little. The happier someone is, the more their eyes narrow. Add a glint to each eye.

SAD

Sketch the mouth turned down a bit. Draw the eyebrows at an angle and make the eyes small, as if partially closed.

ANGRY

Draw the eyes wide open with the whites showing. Add pointed eyebrows above. Draw an open mouth with lots of teeth showing!

CONFUSED

Confused and worried expressions look quite similar. Draw a furrow between the eyebrows and make the bottom lip droop a bit. The top teeth can be biting the lower lip too.

SURPRISED

Draw big oval shapes for the eyes, showing both the irises and whites of the eyes. Raise up the eyebrows and round the mouth. Imagine someone saying 'OOH'!

LAUGHING

Sketch arched eyebrows. Use curved lines for shut eyes. Draw an open mouth showing the top row of teeth. Tilt the head back a bit for a hearty laugh.

ANIMALS IN CLOTHES

1

TO DRAW A DOG, SKETCH OVALS FOR THE HEAD AND FEET, CIRCLES FOR THE CHEST, REAR AND JOINTS AND LINES FOR THE BACK AND LEGS, AS SHOWN.

2

START OUTLINING THE DOG'S BODY SHAPE, GOING AROUND THE GUIDELINES, AS SHOWN. THEN SKETCH THE EARS AND TAIL.

3

JOIN THE SHAPES TOGETHER USING A STRONGER OUTLINE TO BRING OUT THE REAL CONTOUR OF THE DOG'S BODY.

4

RUB AWAY THE GUIDELINES, THEN DRAW THE DOG'S FACIAL FEATURES, TOES AND CLAWS. ADD A ZIG-ZAG PATTERNED JUMPER.

Adding more water to your paints will give a diluted, wash-like effect.

5

USE WATERCOLOUR PAINTS TO COLOUR THE DOG AND JUMPER. CHOOSE BRIGHT COLOURS FOR THE JUMPER TO MAKE IT STAND OUT FROM THE DOG'S DARK FUR. ADD SOME LIGHT AND DARK SHADING FOR DEPTH AND TEXTURE.

GO CRAZY DRAWING OTHER ANIMALS IN FUNNY CLOTHES AND ACCESSORIES!

DOG IN A TIE

Go for a small, smiley dog with a little tongue and short, scratchy fur.

Draw a basic tie shape with a sophisticated striped pattern.

Or try giving this handsome pooch a bow tie!

PENGUIN IN A TOP HAT

Sketch a circle for the penguin's head and an oval for the body. Add an eye, beak and flippers.

Create a 3D top hat using a cylinder. Curve up the hat's brim for this cheeky chappy. Don't forget the feather!

CAT IN GLASSES

Draw your basic cat. Then add a pair of glasses - the bigger the better for the fun factor! Go for solid frames too.

Link rectangle shapes together to draw the hamster's blingy necklace.

HAMSTER WITH BLING

Use oval shapes to draw a hamster. Add facial features and define the little fingers and toes.

109

WATERFALL

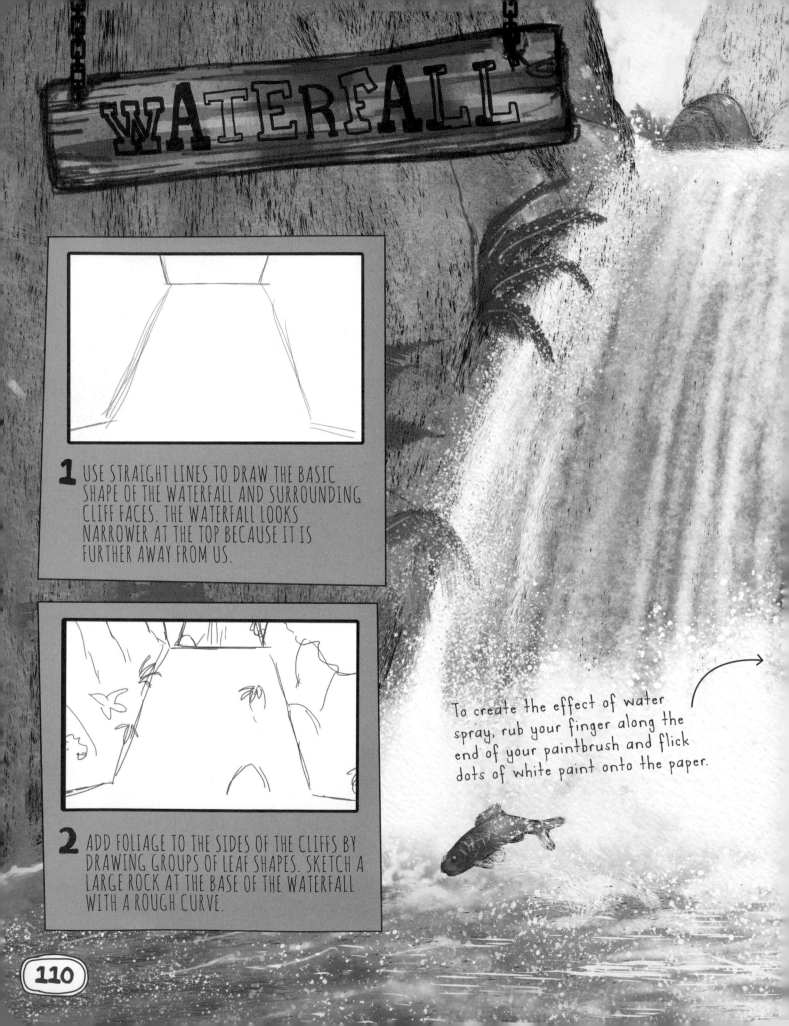

1 USE STRAIGHT LINES TO DRAW THE BASIC SHAPE OF THE WATERFALL AND SURROUNDING CLIFF FACES. THE WATERFALL LOOKS NARROWER AT THE TOP BECAUSE IT IS FURTHER AWAY FROM US.

2 ADD FOLIAGE TO THE SIDES OF THE CLIFFS BY DRAWING GROUPS OF LEAF SHAPES. SKETCH A LARGE ROCK AT THE BASE OF THE WATERFALL WITH A ROUGH CURVE.

To create the effect of water spray, rub your finger along the end of your paintbrush and flick dots of white paint onto the paper.

Use watery paint so that the bands of colour bleed into each other, giving the impression of movement.

3 USING A PEN OR PENCIL, ADD SOME SURFACE DETAIL TO THE GUSHING WATER AND CLIFF FACES. KEEPING YOUR STROKES SHORT, SKETCH LOTS OF SHORT LINES.

4 TO COLOUR THE WATERFALL, USE A DEEP BLUE AS A BASE TONE, THEN PAINT VERTICAL BANDS OF PALER BLUES ON TOP, ALONG WITH STREAKS OF WHITE.

5 USE DIFFERENT SHADES OF BLUE FOR THE POOL AT THE BOTTOM OF THE WATERFALL. ADD HIGHLIGHTS TO THE SURFACE OF THE WATER BY PAINTING LOTS OF THIN, HORIZONTAL LINES.

HELICOPTER

1

START WITH SIMPLE SHAPES. DRAW THREE
ROUNDED RECTANGLES FOR THE CABIN, A LONG
TUBE WITH A TRIANGLE AT THE END FOR THE TAIL
AND AN OVAL ON TOP FOR THE ROTOR BLADES.

2

ADD MORE SIMPLE SHAPES TO THE
TAIL AND ROTORS, AS SHOWN.
DRAW ROUNDED WINDOWS AND
SKETCH THE LANDING SKIDS.

3

REFINE YOUR OUTLINES AND RUB OUT THE
CONSTRUCTION SHAPES. ADD SMALLER
DETAILS, SUCH AS AN OVAL FOR THE TAIL
ROTOR AND SMALL CIRCLES FOR THE LIGHTS.

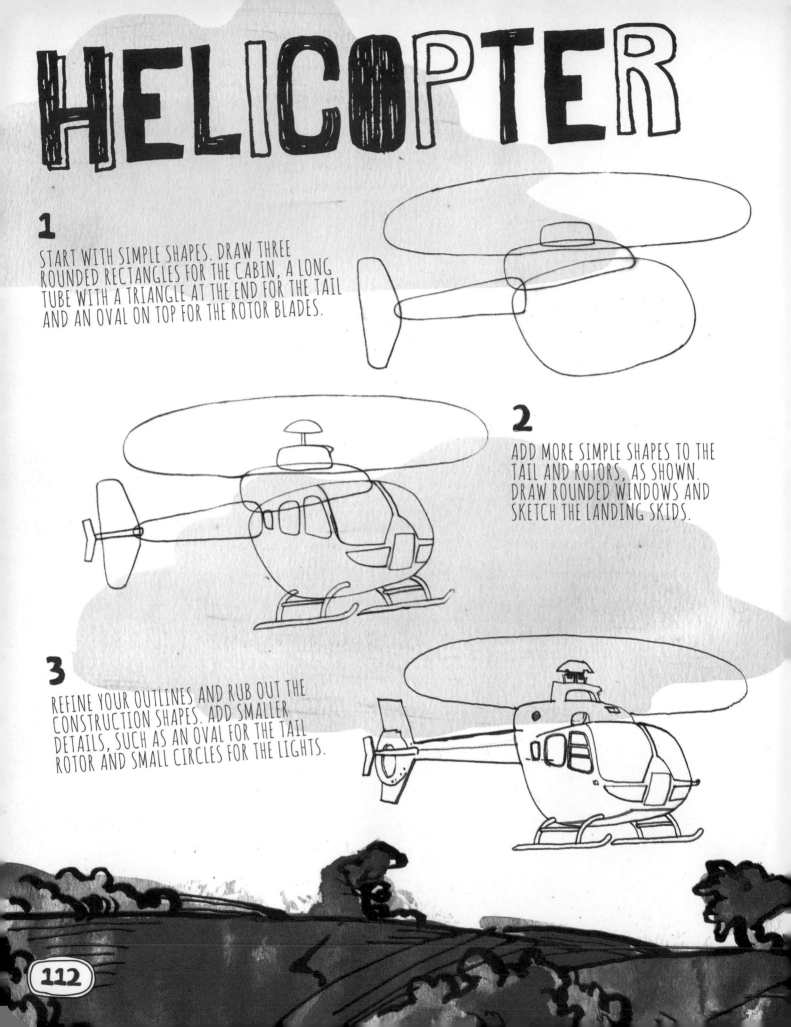

4

TRACE OVER YOUR DRAWING IN BLACK INK. USE WAVY LINES TO CREATE THE IMPRESSION OF FAST, SPINNING BLADES. ADD REFLECTIONS TO THE WINDOWS USING MORE WAVY LINES.

Enhance the sense of movement by colouring the wavy rotor lines in a bluey-grey shade.

5

PAINT THE HELICOPTER IN A BRIGHT COLOUR. USE A BLUE WASH FOR THE WINDOWS, AS IF THEY'RE REFLECTING THE SKY. PICK OUT THE WAVY REFLECTIONS IN A LIGHTER TONE.

Draw lots of gentle curves to create a simple landscape below. Colour with patches of yellow and green watercolours.

KEYS

1

DRAW A LONG, THIN CYLINDER SHAPE FOR THE KEY SHAFT. THEN SKETCH ROUGH RECTANGULAR SHAPES FOR THE HEAD AND TAIL.

2

ADD OVAL AND RECTANGULAR SHAPES TO THE SHAFT, A CIRCLE AND SEMI-CIRCLE TO THE TOP AND ANGULAR RIDGES AT THE BOTTOM FOR AN OLD-FASHIONED KEY STYLE.

Simple swirls and patterns will give the key an ornate effect.

Use crosshatching on the large, flat sections.

3

RUB OUT ANY GUIDELINES AND START SHADING THE KEY USING GENTLE PENCIL STROKES.

4

GO OVER ANY DARKER AREAS ON THE KEY WITH ANOTHER LAYER OF SHADING. USE AN ERASER TO CREATE AREAS WITH HIGHLIGHTS.

When shading cylinder shapes, follow the length using smooth, evenly pressured pencil marks.

NAIL ART

1 USE YOUR HANDS (OR A FRIEND'S) AS A CANVAS AND PAINT A PLAIN BACKGROUND COLOUR ON EACH NAIL.

2 DRAW THREE CHEVRONS STARTING FROM THE NAIL TIP, USING A NEW SHADE.

3 IN ANOTHER COLOUR, REPEAT THE PATTERN IN THE OPPOSITE DIRECTION.

4 FINISH WITH THE SAME PATTERN ON EITHER SIDE OF THE NAIL, USING DIFFERENT COLOURS AGAIN.

3 PAINT DOTS, SWITCHING THE COLOURS YOU USED FOR THE BACKGROUND.

4 DRAW A DARK OUTLINE AROUND THE DOTS TO MAKE THEM POP OUT.

2 ADD A CONTRASTING COLOUR AT THE BOTTOM OF THE NAIL.

1 COLOUR THE BACKGROUND TWO THIRDS OF THE WAY DOWN FROM THE NAIL TIP.

1 COLOUR THE NAIL IN A LIGHT SHADE.

2 PAINT TWO THIN TRIANGLES ON EITHER SIDE OF THE NAIL IN BLACK, AS SHOWN.

3 PAINT A TINY BOW TIE NEAR THE CUTICLE.

4 ADD TWO BLACK DOTS FOR BUTTONS DOWN THE CENTRE OF THE NAIL TO FINISH A TUXEDO PATTERN.

CREATE MORE NAIL PATTERNS USING SIMPLE SHAPES...

HEARTS AND SPOTS
Decorate a simple heart shape with tiny spots in and around the heart.

ZIG-ZAGS
Experiment with thick and thin zig-zags for a lively-looking pattern.

STARS
Try painting glitzy stars in a variety of sizes and colours.

DOTS
Overlapping dots in different colours and shades create a pretty confetti-like appearance.

BIPLANE

1 DRAW A LONG BREAD-LIKE SHAPE, WITH A CURVE AT THE BOTTOM. TAPER OFF THE ENDS, THEN ADD TWO ROUNDED LINES IN THE CENTRE AND ANOTHER AT THE FRONT, LIKE THIS.

2 SKETCH AN OVAL SHAPE FOR THE VERTICAL TAIL AT THE BACK OF THE PLANE. ADD ROUNDED RECTANGLES FOR THE WINGS AND HORIZONTAL TAIL. DRAW A CIRCLE FOR THE PROPELLOR AT THE FRONT AND MORE LINES ON THE BODY.

3 FOR THE WING SUPPORTS AND PROPELLOR BLADES, DRAW LONG RECTANGLE SHAPES. SKETCH OVAL-SHAPED WHEELS, THEN ADD THE ENGINE COMPONENTS, USING OVALS AND RECTANGLES, ONTO THE BIPLANE'S BODY.

4 FILL IN MORE DETAIL USING STRAIGHT LINES, CIRCLES AND RECTANGLES, AS SHOWN. CREATE A PILOT USING AN OVAL FOR THE HEAD AND CURVED LINES FOR THE SHOULDERS.

5

ADD STRAIGHT LINES ON THE WINGS AND TAIL. SKETCH CURVED LINES BEHIND THE PILOT FOR THE COCKPIT AND AROUND THE PROPELLOR TO SUGGEST MOTION. GIVE YOUR PILOT SOME GOGGLES, A HELMET AND A FLOWING SCARF.

Create bullseye markings using circles and ovals.

To make the wings look more 3D, add a thin dark shadow along the bottom.

6

USE OPAQUE (THICK) OR ACRYLIC PAINT TO COLOUR YOUR DRAWING. ADD LIGHT AND DARK SHADING ON THE AIRCRAFT AND PILOT. FINISH WITH A SPOTTY SCARF FOR THE PILOT AND A STRIPY PATTERN ON THE HORIZONTAL AND VERTICAL TAILS FOR CHARACTER.

Smudge the paint with a fat brush to make the propellor look like it's spinning fast.

SPRING

CREATE A SUNNY SPRINGTIME PARK SCENE, FULL OF LOOSE PENCIL AND PAINT STROKES FOR A LIGHT FEEL.

Draw a stick figure, then flesh it out. If you're stuck for ideas, leaf through fashion magazines for inspiration!

For tree blossom, sketch groups of five leaves. When you paint the leaves, use rough splodges of colour. To get the texture of tree bark, use a pencil to make short, sketchy strokes.

Use lots of short, delicate pencil marks to create a feathery texture on birds.

Use both light and heavy shading to give your sketch character and depth. Draw random, wiggly lines on the skirt for a cool, light print.

Draw daffodils with six petals. From the side, the middle part looks trumpet shaped.

Draw some blossom on the ground, as if it's just fallen from the trees. Try drawing the flowers at different angles and add some random leaves as well.

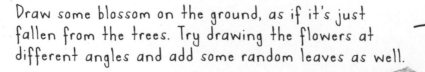

Leave some areas white when you paint the picture, to create the effect of bright, glimmering sunlight!

SUMMER

NOTHING SAYS SUMMER MORE THAN SANDY BEACHES, BRIGHT GREEN LEAVES AND CLEAR, SUNNY SKIES!

Sketch the sun shape with a light pencil, using a ruler to draw the shapes of the sunbeams. If you place the sun high in the sky, the shadows it casts will look short and it will feel like super-sunny midday.

Paint the leaves on the trees in light shades of green. Use a pale yellow around the edges of the treetops to show the sun's highlights.

Sketch a figure wearing a light summer outfit. Add movement where you can - you could draw hair blowing in the breeze, a flowing skirt or a puppy pulling on its lead!

Give some of your figures a tasty ice-cream or lollipop. Draw your outlines with 'U' shapes at the bottom to give the impression they're melting in the heat!

To draw someone on a bike, it's easiest to sketch the bike frame and wheels first. Then add someone riding it.

AUTUMN

USE LOTS OF BROWNS, YELLOWS AND ORANGES TO CREATE
THE FEEL OF AN AUTUMNAL SCENE.

Trees lose their leaves in the autumn, so sketch them with
lots of bare branches. Notice how the branches themselves
split into narrower ones. Try not to make your tree too neat
and tidy - a few imperfections make it look more natural!

In your picture,
scatter a few fallen
acorns on the ground.
The upper part of an
acorn is dome-shaped,
with a rounded
section underneath.
Create texture with
lots of tiny curves.

Leaves come in all sorts of shapes and sizes! Add
falling leaves to your picture to create a sense
of movement. Colour the treetops with areas of
orange and brown, then add lots of blobs in earthy
tones to represent the hundreds of leaves.

WINTER

IT'S EASY TO SET A WINTER SCENE – LANDSCAPES SUDDENLY LOOK DIFFERENT WHEN THEY'RE COVERED IN SNOW AND ICICLES!

Sketch the basic shape of a snowman by drawing three different-sized circles on top of each other. Create character by adding tiny details.

Include action poses when you can in scenes. Here, sketch someone with his weight on his back foot and his arm up, ready to throw a snowball!

Draw trees using long wavy lines for the bare branches. Add vertical, wavy lines for bark. For hanging icicles, draw sharp 'V' shapes.

Use a few simple wavy lines here and there to give the impression of mounds of snow. Add watery blue washes near the figures to create subtle shadows. Give yellow glows around lights to stand out against the wintery blue sky.

CHAISE LONGUE

1

DRAW A CIRCLE FOR THE UPPER BACK OF THE CHAISE AND RECTANGLES FOR THE SEAT, LOWER BACK AND LEGS.

2

ADD TWO ROUGH GUIDES FOR ARMRESTS ON EITHER END OF THE SEAT, AS SHOWN.

Keep the linework soft and fluid to give the chair a luxurious appearance.

Use curved, swirly lines on the legs and framework to suggest carved wood, and straight lines for stitching and creases.

3

JOIN THE SHAPES TOGETHER WITH A SMOOTH, STRONGER OUTLINE, ADDING CURVES AROUND THE EDGES AND TWO ROUNDED FEET.

4

RUB AWAY THE GUIDELINES AND START ADDING IN MORE DETAIL, SUCH AS THE CUSHION AND DECORATIVE ELEMENTS.

5
SET THE SCENE FOR YOUR CHAISE LONGUE BY ADDING IN SOME BACKGROUND DETAIL, LIKE A CHANDELIER AND RUG. THEN ADD VINTAGE COLOUR! USE DIFFERENT SHADES OF THE SAME COLOUR FOR SOPHISTICATED, CHIC STYLE.

Draw a 1920s flapper girl - and her cat! - to add authentic personality to your picture.

Give your room a homey appearance with a small, curvy table and a colourful vase of flowers.

ALIENS

TRY OUT DIFFERENT TYPES OF BODY PARTS TO CREATE ALL KINDS OF BIZARRE ALIEN BEINGS. JUST USE YOUR IMAGINATION!

BODY

1

GET SOME IDEAS BY LOOKING AT THE BODY SHAPES OF HUMANS AND UNUSUAL ANIMALS. EVEN PLANTS CAN GIVE YOU INSPIRATION!

LEGS

2

DESIGN THE LEGS. A LARGE ALIEN MIGHT HAVE SHORTER, FATTER LEGS, WHILE A MORE ATHLETIC CREATURE COULD HAVE LONG, SPINDLY ONES.

ARMS

3

IT'S EASY TO DRAW ODD-LOOKING LIMBS. FOR EXAMPLE, YOU COULD DRAW A CRAB'S CLAW ATTACHED TO A FROG'S ARM. IT'S UP TO YOU!

HEADS

4

THE SHAPE OF YOUR ALIEN'S HEAD AFFECTS HOW AGGRESSIVE OR CLEVER IT LOOKS. A BIG SKULL SUGGESTS A BIG BRAIN. A BIG JAW SUGGESTS FIERCENESS!

MOUTHS

5

MOUTH SHAPES ALSO AFFECT YOUR CREATURE'S PERCEPTION. BIG LIPS AND FUNNY TEETH LOOK HARMLESS AND SILLY, WHEREAS HUGE, SPIKY FANGS LOOK REALLY SCARY!

EYES

6

GIVE YOUR ALIEN AS MANY EYES AS YOU LIKE. BIG EYES WILL MAKE IT LOOK CUTER AND MORE CHILDLIKE. SMALLER OR NARROWED EYES WILL MAKE IT LOOK MEAN AND ANGRY.

URBAN ART

COMBINE SIMPLE SHAPES AND EXCITING PAINT
EFFECTS TO CREATE YOUR OWN URBAN ART.

STENCILS

Cut out a shape, lay it onto
some paper, then flick ink
or paint all over it. Remove
the stencil to reveal the
shape underneath!

Experiment with different paint
techniques, such as splashing or
spraying within the stencil.

STIPPLING

Load a bristle brush with paint
and flick it onto some paper.
Practise to work out how much
water to use - too much will
make the splats too big.

Or, spread some paint thinly on a
plate. Dip a sponge into it then dab
the sponge onto paper.

COLOUR SHADING

Create a cool colour gradient by
bleeding one watercolour tone into
another. Wet the paper first.

3D SHAPES

Make a star look 3D by sketching curves trailing
away from it, gradually becoming closer together.

To add to the 3D effect, think about where the light
source is and add areas of shadow in solid black.

CREATING URBAN ART

Practise drawing simple shapes on their own. Use hearts, flames, wings - whatever you like! Give them thick outlines so they stand out.

3D HEART

WING

TWISTED ROPE

SPLAT HEART

Then bring all your shapes together to create an amazing piece of artwork with lots of overlapping layers. Use different paint techniques to create a riot of colour and a real sense of movement!

133

DOORS AND WINDOWS

YOU CAN USE ALL SORTS OF SHAPES AND PATTERNS TO DRAW ORNATE DOORS AND WINDOWS. HAVE FUN!

HOUSE FRONT DOORS

First, decide the basic shape of your door. Draw rectangles for the door itself, plus any panels or door posts. Then add details such as arches, handles and ornamental decoration.

OTHER DOORS

Try drawing other types of doors. A castle entrance could have a simple arch shape, while a temple door could look more unusual. Some doors look quite plain, while others can have beautiful markings.

CASTLE DOOR

TEMPLE DOOR

STABLE DOOR

WINDOW SHAPES

Build up the shapes of windows using rectangles, squares and curves. To make the glass look reflective, first paint it light grey, then wash away bands of colour with a clean brush.

RECTANGULAR

ROUNDED

PATTERNED

WINDOW FRAMES

Window frames can look more interesting than the actual windows! Use curls, swirls and other patterns to give your windows beautifully decorated borders.

DECORATIVE WINDOW

CHURCH WINDOW

WROUGHT IRON

STAINED GLASS

Stained-glass windows have amazing multicoloured patterns. Paint them using watercolours, as if the sunlight is shining through.

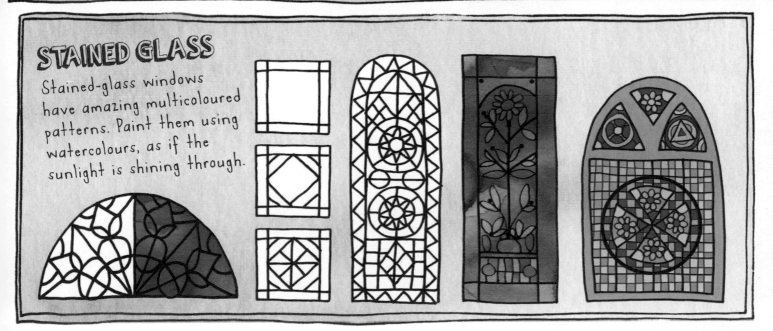

SKELETON

1

SKETCH AN OVAL FOR THE HEAD, CIRCLES FOR THE SHOULDERS, ELBOWS AND KNEES AND LINES FOR THE BASIC BODY FRAME.

2

ADD GUIDELINES, TRIANGLES AND CIRCLES, READY TO POSITION THE EYES, NOSE, MOUTH, RIB CAGE AND PELVIS, AS SHOWN.

3

USING THE SHAPES AND GUIDELINES, DRAW THE OUTLINE OF THE SKELETON. ADD CYLINDER SHAPES FOR THE HANDS AND FEET.

4

NOW SKETCH IN ALL THE BONE SHAPES, USING OVALS, RECTANGLES, TRIANGLES AND CURVED LINES, LIKE THIS.

For the rib cage, draw the central bone first then add the ribs one side at a time.

Draw three cylinder-shaped segments for each finger and toe.

Cranium

Clavicle

Humerus

Ribs

Vertebrae

Radius

Ulna

Pelvis

Phalanges

5

COLOUR THE SKELETON, ADDING DARKER SHADING AROUND THE BONES AND BEHIND THE RIB CAGE.

Femur

Patella

Tibia

Tarsals

Fibula

Phalanges

137

CAMOUFLAGE PATTERNS

EXPERIMENT WITH DIFFERENT SHAPES AND COLOURS TO CREATE THESE COOL CAMO DESIGNS!

COMBAT STYLE

DRAW LOTS OF INTERLOCKING SHAPES AS SHOWN. COLOUR WITH DIFFERENT SHADES OF GREEN AND BROWN.

DESERT STYLE

SKETCH MORE COMPLICATED SHAPES, BUT USE A SIMPLE TWO-TONE COLOUR SCHEME, SUCH AS BEIGE AND KHAKI.

NAVY STYLE

CREATE THE EFFECT OF RIPPLING WATER USING FOUR CONTRASTING BLUE TONES

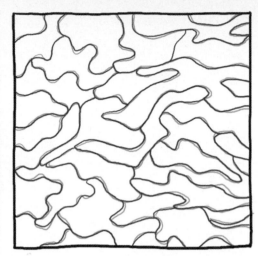

EXPERIMENT WITH DIFFERENT DESIGNS. THIS PATTERN USES A LOT OF SMALLER, LONGER INTERLOCKING SHAPES.

CREATE A JUNGLE-STYLE CAMOUFLAGE BY COLOURING YOUR PATTERN WITH FOUR DIFFERENT SHADES OF GREEN.

USE HOOPS AND LOOPS TO CREATE SHAPES THAT LOOK MORE ROUNDED – AND MORE FUN!

YOU DON'T ALWAYS HAVE TO USE EARTHY TONES. BRIGHT AND BOLD COLOURS CAN WORK REALLY WELL TOO.

USE NATURE AS INSPIRATION. EVEN SEAWEED SHAPES WORK WELL!

USE VARYING NEUTRAL TONES WITH A SINGLE ACCENT COLOUR FOR IMPACT.

1

DRAW A TALL CYLINDER SHAPE WITH A POINTED TIP. ADD TWO SIMILAR, BUT THINNER, SHAPES ON EITHER SIDE, THEN A THIRD SHORTER SIMILAR SHAPE IN FRONT.

2

DRAW THE OUTLINE OF THE SPACE SHUTTLE AND ADD ITS CURVED DOORS. DRAW CURVES ON THE TWO BOOSTERS AND FUEL TANK TO MAKE THEM LOOK MORE 3D.

3

DRAW EXTRA CURVED BANDS ON THE ROCKET BOOSTERS, PLUS OTHER DETAILS AT THE TOP. ADD MORE LINES ON THE WINGS, FOLLOWING THE CURVED SHAPE OF EACH ONE.

Don't forget to add astronauts in space suits, walking towards their shuttle and mission!

Use narrow bands of white and light grey to help give the shuttle and its boosters a shiny, metallic look.

Notice how the bottom part of the shuttle reflects the fiery rocket flames!

4

SKETCH MORE CURVED LINES ON THE SIDES OF THE BOOSTERS AND ON THE EXHAUST SECTION OF THE SHUTTLE. ADD MORE SMALL SURFACE DETAILS, SUCH AS THE SHUTTLE'S CABIN WINDOWS.

5

COLOUR THE FUEL TANK ORANGE AND PAINT THE BOOSTERS AND SPACE SHUTTLE WHITE. ADD LONG BANDS OF VARYING GREY TONES TO ADD DEPTH TO THE SHUTTLE.

PINEAPPLE PRINT

LEARN TO DRAW A PINEAPPLE, THEN CREATE STYLISTIC VARIATIONS FOR COOL PATTERNS AND PRINTS.

1 FOR A BASIC PINEAPPLE, START BY SKETCHING AN OVAL SHAPE.

2 DRAW CRISS-CROSSING LINES CURVING ACROSS THE OVAL. ADD POINTY LEAF SHAPES AT THE TOP.

Try a simpler, stylistic variation of your pineapple. Copy this pineapple onto tracing paper. Turn over the tracing paper and use the back of a spoon to rub and print the pineapple onto plain paper. Repeat the print across the plain paper at angles. Go over each pineapple with a pen then colour.

Triangle shapes give the impression of leaves folding over.

3

GO OVER THE PENCIL MARKS WITH A WATERPROOF PEN AND THICKEN THE CRISS-CROSS LINES. ADD MORE LEAF SHAPES.

Follow the shape of the leaves when shading.

4

USE A MOSTLY VERTICAL SHADING TECHNIQUE ON EACH LEAF AND DIAMOND FOR A 3D EFFECT.

This time, create a more detailed drawing of a pineapple, using a mixture of thick, thin, straight and wavy lines. Apply the same printing technique as on the opposite page. Rotate the pineapple print to make a pattern suitable for gift wrap or even clothing fabric! Try cool colours.

POINTILLISM

IN THIS DRAWING STYLE, PICTURES ARE MADE OUT OF LOTS OF LITTLE DOTS.

1
START WITH A PHOTO OF A FACE THEN TRACE OVER IT WITH SOFT PENCIL LINES. ONLY DRAW THE SHAPES OF THE MAIN FACIAL FEATURES AT THIS STAGE.

2
ADD SOME DETAILS. DEFINE THE SHAPES OF THE EARS, EYES, NOSE AND CHIN, THEN ADD A LITTLE SHADING FOR THE HAIR.

3
GO OVER THE DRAWING WITH AN INK PEN, MAKING LOTS OF SMALL DOTS. NEXT, LIGHTLY DRAW A PENCIL OUTLINE TO SEPARATE THE MAIN AREAS OF LIGHT AND DARK IN THE IMAGE.

4
SHADE IN THE DARKEST AREAS OF THE FACE AND NECK USING LOTS OF DOTS DRAWN VERY CLOSE TOGETHER.

5

LEAVE THE LIGHTER AREAS OF THE FACE WHITE. TO ADD MORE SUBTLE SHADING, VARY THE QUANTITY OF DOTS YOU USE, AS WELL AS THE AMOUNT OF SPACING BETWEEN THEM.

SAILBOAT

1 DRAW TWO BASIC TRIANGLES FOR THE SAILS, THEN A LONG CURVED SHAPE WITH A HOOK FOR THE TOP OF THE BOAT, AS SHOWN.

2 SKETCH THIN CYLINDER SHAPES AT THE TOP AND SIDES OF THE SAILS AND BOAT. DRAW A RECTANGULAR-SHAPED CABIN UNDER THE SAILS.

Add small overlapping shapes to start creating splashy waves.

3 ATTACH A LONG FLAG POLE TO THE MAST, THEN DRAW ROPE RINGS ON THE MAST AND SPAR. ADD A SMALL CYLINDER AT THE FRONT OF THE BOAT AND MAKE RAILINGS USING LONG AND SHORT LINES.

4 DRAW A WAVY, FLAPPY FLAG, AND ADD ROPES TO JOIN THE SAILS TO THE BOAT. SKETCH SMALL CIRCLES AND RECTANGLES ON THE ROPES TO CREATE THE APPEARANCE OF RIGGING.

Add slightly curved lines in each corner of the sails for material creases and tension.

Smooth curved lines suggest rolling waves.

146

5 DRAW SOME WAVY LINES ON THE SAILS FOR MOVEMENT AND TO SUGGEST WHERE THE MATERIAL HAS BEEN JOINED TOGETHER. SKETCH MORE ROLLING WAVES TO THE FRONT OF THE BOAT.

6 ADD SHORT WIGGLY LINES ON THE SAILS FOR TIES. NOW PAINT THE PICTURE, APPLYING A LIGHT, FADE-AWAY TECHNIQUE ON THE SAILS FOR A 3D EFFECT.

For the background, use a smooth watercolour wash so the boat pops against the soft horizon.

A curved line on the hull or outside of the boat gives the impression of wooden planks.

CIRCUS

Larger elements at the top of the tent give the scene a sense of scale and depth.

1

TO DRAW A BASIC CIRCUS RING, SKETCH TWO OVERLAPPING OVAL SHAPES USING SIMPLE PERSPECTIVE, AS SHOWN.

2

CREATE PEOPLE IN THE AUDIENCE USING CIRCLES AND SEMI-CIRCLES. DRAW CURVED LINES FOR THE TOP OF THE TENT AND ADD A STAR IN THE RING.

3

SKETCH LOOSER LINES AROUND EACH AUDIENCE MEMBER AND ADD MORE PEOPLE! DRAW ROUNDED SEMI-RECTANGLES AT THE BACK OF THE AUDIENCE FOR SEATING.

Make the audience members in the foreground bigger than those in the background to add to the perspective.

To build up the audience, draw overlapping people, like this. Give each person a different hairstyle for individuality.

Circus acts in and above the ring add to the action and story of your picture.

4

DRAW EVEN MORE PEOPLE IN THE AUDIENCE, AND ADD THE RINGMASTER, CLOWN AND TRAPEZE ARTIST. DRAW SOME LIGHTS AT THE TOP OF THE TENT AND BALLOONS IN THE CROWD. USE WATERCOLOUR PAINTS TO FINISH.

GOLDEN GATE BRIDGE

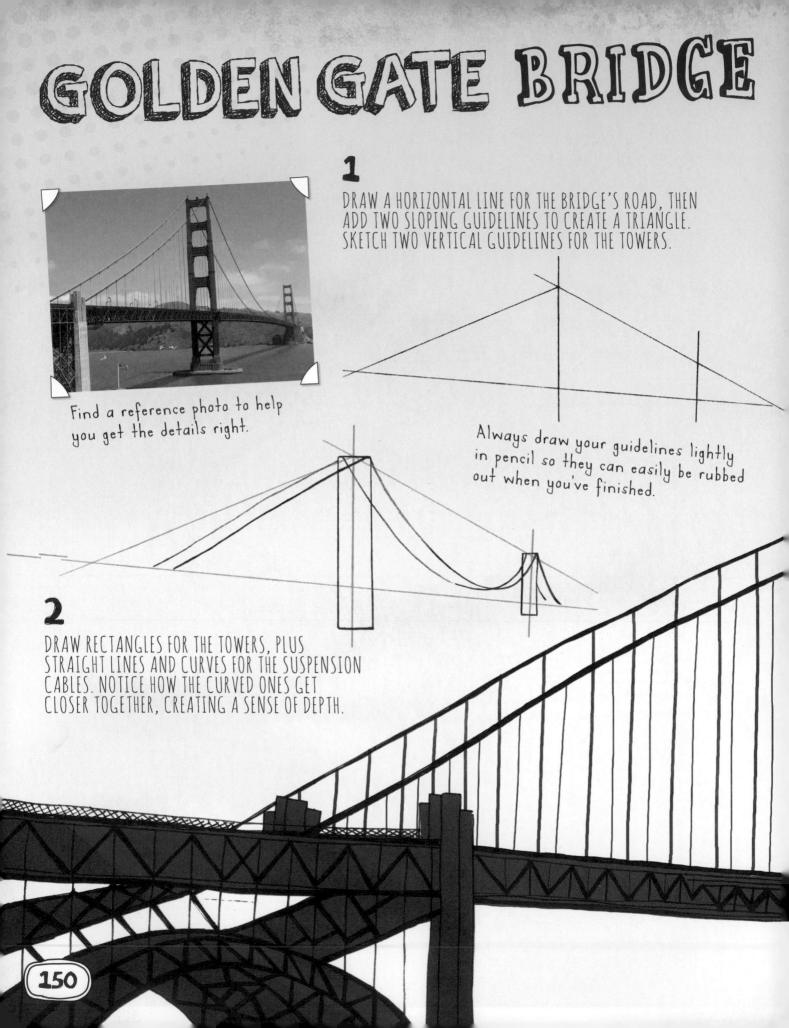

Find a reference photo to help you get the details right.

1

DRAW A HORIZONTAL LINE FOR THE BRIDGE'S ROAD, THEN ADD TWO SLOPING GUIDELINES TO CREATE A TRIANGLE. SKETCH TWO VERTICAL GUIDELINES FOR THE TOWERS.

Always draw your guidelines lightly in pencil so they can easily be rubbed out when you've finished.

2

DRAW RECTANGLES FOR THE TOWERS, PLUS STRAIGHT LINES AND CURVES FOR THE SUSPENSION CABLES. NOTICE HOW THE CURVED ONES GET CLOSER TOGETHER, CREATING A SENSE OF DEPTH.

3

START BUILDING UP MORE OF THE BRIDGE'S STRUCTURE. ADD ROUNDED SQUARES ON THE CENTRE TOWER AND A CURVE AND RECTANGLE FOR THE ARCH ON THE LEFT.

4

NOW FOCUS ON THE FINE DETAILS. USE ZIG-ZAG LINES FOR THE SIDES OF THE BRIDGE AND THE ARCH. ADD EXTRA PARALLEL LINES FOR THE VERTICAL SUSPENSION ROPES.

For a greater sense of perspective, add more detail to the areas of your drawing that are in the foreground.

When you're happy with your pencil sketch, go over it again using waterproof inks.

5

ADD MORE CABLES AND TOWER DETAILS TO YOUR DRAWING, THEN START COLOURING! USE A BLUE WATERCOLOUR WASH FOR THE SKY AND LEAVE TO DRY. FINALLY, PAINT THE BRIDGE IN STRONG ORANGE AND RED TONES.

Use darker shades for the parts of the bridge that are in the distance. Lighter tones suggest areas that are in direct sunlight.

FEATHERS

1 SKETCH THREE OVERLAPPING ROUGH OVALS. THEN ADD A THIN, CURVED STICK DOWN THE CENTRE FOR THE FEATHER'S SHAFT AND QUILL.

2 DRAW A WAVY OUTLINE AROUND THE OVAL SHAPES, ADDING GAPS AND SPIKY BITS FOR A FEATHERY OUTER TEXTURE. RUB AWAY THE GUIDELINES.

3 ADD LOTS OF CURVED LINES FOR THE BARBS, LEADING FROM THE SHAFT OUTWARDS. DON'T MAKE THEM TOO PERFECT – SOME CAN EVEN CURVE BACKWARDS! FINISH WITH COLOUR AND SHADING.

PEACOCK FEATHER
Start with a lollipop shape. Add wavy barbs around the outside and an oval and pie shape in the middle. Colour with rich greens, yellows and blues.

shaft

quill

barbs

152

BLACK AND WHITE
Use a black ink pen to draw the feather shape, then block in some of the barbs at the base using heavier strokes. Leave the other barbs white.

SPOTTY
To create a spotty feather, add some coloured ovals and semi-circular shapes. Sketch lighter lines inside the spots to contrast with the barbs outside, making your pattern stand out.

STRIPY
Use fewer barb lines and add thick coloured rectangular stripes for this eyecatching pattern.

FLUFFY
For a fluffy, floaty feather, sketch soft curvy barb lines in just a slightly darker shade of the main colour. Use your black ink for the outline, shaft and quill only.

CENTAUR

1

USE STRAIGHT AND CURVED LINES TO DRAW A SIMPLE STICK FIGURE LIKE THIS.

2

DRAW CIRCLES AND OVALS TO BUILD UP THE CENTAUR'S BODY SHAPE. THEN SKETCH IN THE ROUGH OUTLINE OF ITS BODY.

3

USE SAUSAGE SHAPES FOR THE LEGS AND SKETCH CIRCLES AND OVALS FOR THE VARIOUS JOINTS. USE LONG, WAVY LINES TO DRAW THE TAIL.

Only start adding detail once you're happy with the basic shapes of the different body parts.

4

START ON THE MORE DETAILED AREAS, SKETCHING IN THE HANDS, HAIR AND FACIAL FEATURES. ADD A BELT, BAG STRAP, HEADBAND AND QUIVER OF ARROWS.

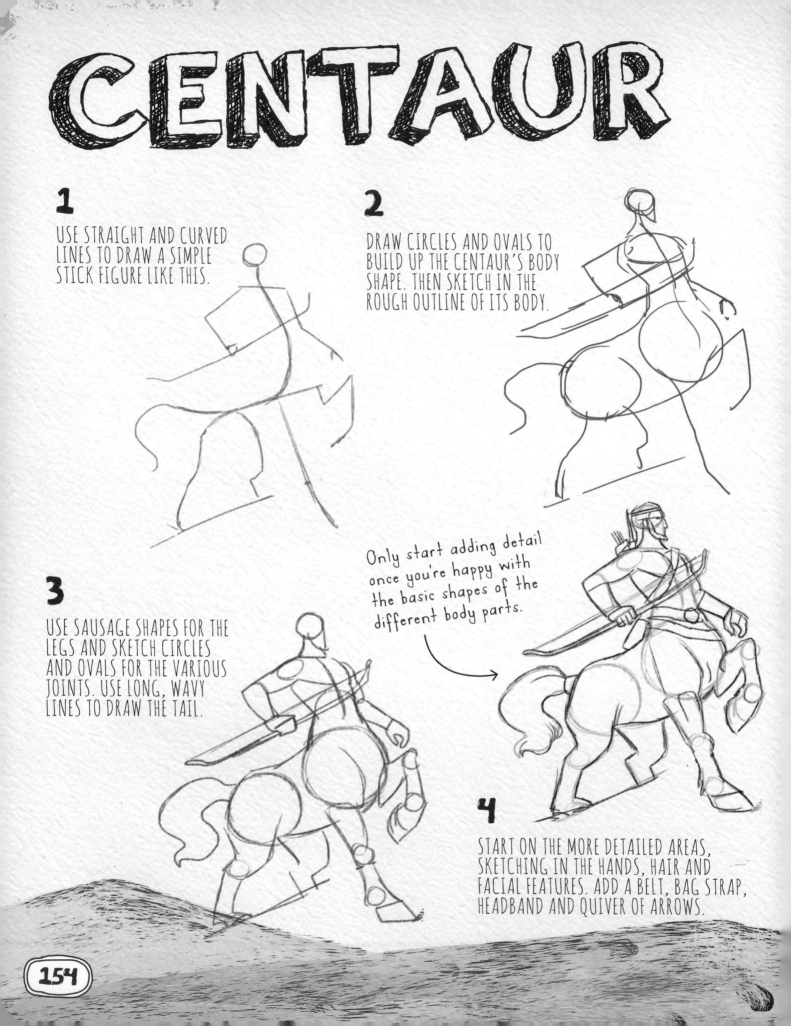

6

TO ADD COLOUR, USE A DARK BROWN FOR THE LOWER BODY, WITH LIGHTER SHADES FOR THE HIGHLIGHTS. PICK A SKIN COLOUR FOR THE FACE AND CHEST, USING DARKER TONES TO HELP DEFINE THE SHAPES OF THE MUSCLES.

5

RUB OUT THE GUIDES. REFINE YOUR PENCIL OUTLINES AND ADD MORE DETAIL TO THE UPPER BODY. USE SHADING TO GIVE THE TAIL AND LOWER BODY A HAIRY TEXTURE.

Use long, wavy, overlapping pencil strokes to create a hairy texture.

KARATE BOY

1

SKETCH CIRCLES FOR THE HEAD, HANDS AND BODY JOINTS, THEN RECTANGLES FOR THE FEET. DRAW STRAIGHT AND CURVED LINES FOR BODY, ARM AND LEG GUIDES. MAKE SURE ONE LEG IS KICKING OUTWARDS!

2

DRAW OVAL SHAPES TO FLESH OUT THE TORSO, ARMS AND LEGS.

3

JOIN THE SHAPES TOGETHER WITH A STRONGER OUTLINE. ADD CLOTHING AND HAIR.

4

RUB AWAY YOUR GUIDELINES TO LEAVE THE OUTLINE OF THE KARATE-KICKING BOY.

5
NOW FOCUS ON THE DETAILS OF YOUR DRAWING. SKETCH IN THE FACIAL FEATURES AND WORK UP THE CLOTHING.

Draw the hair and karate belt at angles for movement and action.

Add shading in the skin tone and on the clothing for depth and texture.

6
ADD A JAPANESE BUILDING IN THE BACKGROUND TO SET THE SCENE FOR YOUR KARATE PICTURE. USE WATERCOLOUR PAINT TO FINISH.

Use darker shades to give an idea of fabric folds. And make sure you give the boy an expert's black belt!

157

TIME MACHINE

BUILD UP SIMPLE SHAPES TO DRAW A CRAZY-LOOKING
CONTRAPTION THAT CAN TRAVEL THROUGH TIME!

FRAMEWORK

First use simple shapes such as ovals and sausages
to create the basic framework of your time machine.

Refine the outline of each section of your
time machine. Start adding surface details to
make it look more mechanical or futuristic.

CIRCUIT

To draw a simple circuit board, sketch a rough rectangle
and add horizontal lines with dots at the ends. Go over
the lines in thick ink pen strokes. Colour the board green.

DIGI CLOCK

Design a clock to show the
year your machine has
travelled to! For the display
screens, use simple rectangle
shapes with round edges.
Use circles for side buttons.

ONCE YOU'VE DESIGNED EACH PART OF YOUR TIME MACHINE, PUT ALL THE DIFFERENT SECTIONS TOGETHER. YOU CAN USE SIMILAR-SHAPED PARTS TO THE ONES SHOWN HERE, OR TRY CREATING YOUR OWN!

Use long, curved lines to draw wires connecting all the different parts together. Colour them with tones of blue for a 3D, tubular feel.

Add darker patches of colour for the areas of the machine that are in shadow. Varying between lighter and darker shades helps add to the 3D look.

1700   1800   1900   2000   2020   AD

HATS

LEARN HOW TO DRAW ALL SORTS OF HATS, THEN HAVE FUN DECORATING THEM WITH DIFFERENT PATTERNS AND TEXTURES.

WHEN YOU DRAW A HAT, REMEMBER THAT THE WEARER'S HEAD WILL AFFECT ITS SHAPE. IT WILL ALSO LOOK DIFFERENT DEPENDING ON THE ANGLE.

CAP SIDE-ON

Try drawing a cap from the side to see its full shape. This one is vaguely dome-shaped with straight sides.

CAP FRONT-ON

When you draw a cap from the front, the peak-shaped brim is more obvious. Some are curved, while others are flatter.

TRILBY STYLE

Don't make the top dent in a trilby hat too deep - remember there's still someone's head underneath it!

WOOLLY

Give the hat trim a woolly texture by drawing a wobbly outline first. Then add lots of tiny curls to it.

BEANIE

When you sketch a beanie, make sure it follows the curved shape of the head, with a bit of extra material sticking up at the top.

WITH GIRLS' HATS, EXPERIMENT WITH AN EVEN WIDER VARIETY OF SHAPES, PATTERNS AND TEXTURES.

Hats will tend to flatten a person's hairstyle, but you'll still see some hair sticking out from underneath!

TEXTURE   Keep your pencil lines quite rough and scratchy to suggest the texture of fabric.

PATTERNS
When you add a pattern to the side of a hat, try to draw it so that it follows the curved shape of the wearer's head.

FLOWER HAT

This rigid-shaped hat is a bit like a cone with the top cut off. Add flowers and bands to decorate.

KNITTED

Use short, faint overlapping lines to make a kind of criss-cross pattern that looks like knitted wool.

SAILOR GIRL

Draw the band first, then used curved lines to draw the puffed shape of the actual hat.

DOT LIZARD

1 USING A RULER, LIGHTLY DRAW A DASHED DIAGONAL LINE. DRAW A SWIRLY LINE ON TOP, AS SHOWN.

2 DRAW AROUND THE SWIRLY LINE TO CREATE THE LIZARD'S HEAD, BODY AND TAIL. SKETCH STICK LEGS AND HANDS AT FUN ANGLES.

3 DRAW AROUND THE STICK LIMBS TO FLESH OUT THE LIZARD'S STUBBY LEGS AND WIDE TOES AND CLAWS.

4 RUB AWAY THE GUIDELINES, THEN USE GOUACHE (A THICK WATERCOLOUR PAINT) TO COLOUR YOUR LIZARD. ONCE DRY, SKETCH WHERE YOU WANT THE DOTS, LINES AND PATTERNS TO GO.

5 USE A FAT FELT-TIP PEN OR MORE GOUACHE PAINT TO COLOUR THE DOTS, LINES AND PATTERNS. HAVE FUN DECORATING YOUR CREATURE!

Paint dots around the lizard too, so that he is part of a patterned ground.

Dot painting consists of various paint colours. These are normally yellow (representing the sun), brown (soil), red (desert) and white (from the clouds and sky).

ABORIGINAL ART

This is a traditional aborigine art method. Long ago, the pictures represented religion and rituals and mostly featured animals and nature.

MASKS

TRADITIONAL MASKS ARE USED IN CEREMONIES, CELEBRATIONS AND RITUALS.

1

SKETCH A LONG OVAL SHAPE, THEN ADD A CURVED, ALMOST SEMI-CIRCULAR SHAPE ON TOP. ADD A CENTRE LINE AS A GUIDE.

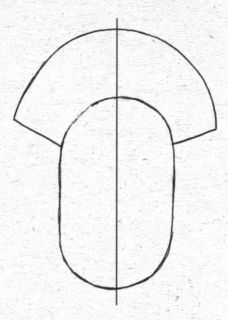

2

DRAW A THIN BORDER INSIDE THE SEMI-CIRCLE. ADD A NOSE, MOUTH AND A SMALL MASK ON THE HEAD. SKETCH SOME TRIANGLES AROUND THE FACE.

3

DRAW STRIPES ON THE HEADDRESS AND FACE. ADD SPIRALS BENEATH THE EYES, THEN SKETCH A FACE ON THE SMALL MASK.

4

COLOUR YOUR MASK IN BRIGHT COLOURS. USE LIGHT AND DARK SHADES IN VERTICAL LINES TO SUGGEST A WOOD-LIKE TEXTURE.

EXPERIMENT WITH DIFFERENT-SHAPED MASKS AND PATTERNS.

SPOTS AND STRIPES
Draw the outline of a mask, then sketch the facial features, making sure each side is symmetrical. Add contrasting patterns, like spots and stripes.

FEATHERS AND DIAGONALS
Sketch a feather shape at the top of your mask and chevrons down the centre. Repeat and fan lots of feathers around the top of the mask.

SHAPES AND CROSSES
Create a mask with eight panels, as shown. Decorate the mask with triangles, circles, diagonals and rectangles.

CLOTHES SHOP

THIS SHOP MIGHT LOOK TRICKY TO DRAW, BUT IT'S MADE UP OF LOTS OF SIMPLER SHAPES.

Draw a clothes rail and add a few hangers. Have fun drawing tops, dresses or skirts - it's up to you!

Draw someone trying on a trendy outfit. Choose a fun, laidback pose.

Practise sketching each object on its own before drawing it in your scene.

Draw the outline of a tailor's dummy - it's basically a person with the head, arms and legs missing! Fill the shape with lots of curves and swirls.

Sketch some simple box shapes with pairs of shoes perched on top. Have a look at fashion mags for inspiration!

Now you can bring everything together! Place the clothes and shoes in the foreground to create a focal point. Draw the girl and dummy higher up the page, to look as if they're further back.

Clothes shops often group similar items together. Try following the same idea as you think about where to put all the different objects.

Add a simple wash for the background and use lots of vibrant colours to really make the clothes stand out!

167

MOUNTAIN RANGE

START BY SKETCHING BASIC TRIANGLE AND RECTANGLE SHAPES AS A GUIDE FOR THE OVERALL LOOK OF YOUR MOUNTAIN RANGE SCENE.

ADD HATCHING LINES, FOLLOWING THE DIRECTION OF THE MOUNTAINS WITH YOUR STROKES. LEAVE THE MOUNTAIN PEAKS WHITE FOR SNOWY TOPS.

USE LIGHT AND HEAVY SHADING TO CREATE DEPTH. SKETCH SPIKY LINES AROUND THE WHITE MOUNTAIN PEAK FOR THE SNOW.

Snow-capped pine trees add to the wintry feel of your drawing. Give the drawing personality with other small details, like a wolf and log cabin.

Give the scene colour! Add some dark hilly land in the distance. Use a light blue wash on the mountain snow for a more realistic, 3D effect.

Use different intensities of colour for contrast and texture.

Darker shades in the background will give an impression of depth and distance.

BEFORE COLOURING, SKETCH A TRAIN, DEER AND LINES TO SUGGEST GRASS AND TEXTURE IN THE TREES AND MOUNTAINS. USE AN INK PEN TO GO OVER ALL YOUR LINES, THEN ADD COLOUR. BUILD UP THE SCENE WITH MORE TREES.

BASEBALL PLAYER

1

USE A LIGHT 2H PENCIL TO DRAW A SIMPLE STICK FIGURE. CONCENTRATE ON THE BASIC POSE, MAKING SURE THE FEET ARE PLANTED CORRECTLY.

2

SKETCH THE VARIOUS BODY PARTS, USING YOUR STICKS AS A GUIDE. FOCUS ON GETTING THE OVERALL SHAPE AND PROPORTIONS RIGHT.

3

NOW ADD A LITTLE DETAIL. LIGHTLY SKETCH THE HELMET AND THE SHAPES OF THE CLOTHES. DRAW THE FINGERS AND ADD ROUGH FACIAL FEATURES.

4

USE A 4B PENCIL TO WORK ON THE FINE DETAILS. SHADE IN AREAS NOT HIT BY YOUR LIGHT SOURCE AND THE FOLDS IN THE CLOTHING.

5

GO OVER YOUR PENCIL LINES WITH A BLACK INK PEN. PAINT THE BASEBALL BAT A LIGHT BROWN AND PICK OUT DETAILS ON THE PLAYER'S CLOTHES IN A BRIGHT, PUNCHY COLOUR.

Draw a baseball and add light horizontal lines to show it's moving super fast!

If you're using watercolours to paint your drawing, leave the outfit white, but use a pale wash to add subtle shadows.

SNOWFLAKES

Draw three lines to make a basic star shape. Sketch a smaller star inside it then add arrow shapes on the bigger star, as shown.

Turn each arrow into a triangle by drawing a line across it. Sketch more arrow shapes and add some diamonds too.

This snowflake is similar to the one above. Don't colour exactly in the lines for a soft effect. Use cool colours like purple and lilac for a wintry feel.

The lilac background and dashed line around the outside of this snowflake give it a flowery-looking variation of the other snowflakes.

For this spotty design, start with the basic star shape, then add circles to the ends of the spikes.

For another variation, add more circles and gradually lighten the colour of them towards the centre.

Change the size, position and amount of circles for a more interesting spotty snowflake.

The dots on this snowflake give it a lacy feel. Shade the edges a darker colour for depth and delicacy.

After the basic star shape design, draw zig-zags around the edge of the snowflake, joining the spikes together. Add a leaf-shaped pattern inside for a heavier flake.

GRIFFIN

1

START WITH SIMPLE OVALS TO SKETCH THE BASIC SHAPE OF YOUR GRIFFIN, AS SHOWN.

2

DRAW MORE ROUGH OVALS FOR THE WINGS, EARS, TOES, EYE AND TAIL END. CREATE A HOOKED, EAGLE-SHAPED BEAK AND A THIN, LION-LIKE TAIL.

3

REPEAT SIMPLE 'U' SHAPES ON THE GRIFFIN'S WINGS AND TORSO FOR A FEATHERY EFFECT. USE A HEAVIER, MORE FLUID LINE TO DRAW AROUND THE EARS, FACE, BODY, LEGS AND CLAWS, TO JOIN THEM TOGETHER.

4

OUTLINE YOUR SKETCH WITH BLACK PEN OR INK. ADD SOME SHADING ON THE TWO LEGS IN THE BACKGROUND. FILL IN MORE DETAIL ON THE BEAK, FACE, EARS AND TAIL. RUB AWAY ANY PENCIL MARKS.

5 ADD SOME SNOW-CAPPED MOUNTAINS IN THE BACKGROUND TO GIVE THE IMPRESSION OF A ROUGH TERRAIN. FINISH WITH WATERCOLOUR PAINT.

Use lighter shades to start, then add darker tones to give your griffin depth and texture.

Draw a loose line beneath the griffin. Colour the area above the line in green and below it in grey to stand your mythical creature on a cliff edge.

THE 1920S

HAIRSTYLES

Use wavy lines to draw this '20s men's hairstyle. Sketch short, straight lines at the sides.

HATS

A straw boater is basically a cylinder attached to a disc shape, with a ribbon and bow. The fedora hat is taller with the top pinched in at the sides.

WAISTCOAT

Draw this waistcoat pattern with rows of fan shapes. Add shaded curved shapes to each one, tapering to a single point.

SHOES

Two-tone and lace-up shoes were trendy in the '20s. Use curved lines for the simple shape of a side-on shoe. Design a pattern using more curves.

HAIRSTYLES

For a straight bob, keep to the head shape then define a straight fringe. For a wavy style, sketch long, flowing lines ending in neat curls by the mouth.

HATS AND BANDS

Women's hats were simple and elegant in the '20s. Add bands and bows to basic hat shapes using curved lines. Colour these elements in contrasting tones.

DRESS

For this dress pattern, draw overlapping diamond shapes in different sizes. You can also try overlapping curves and rectangle shapes.

Instead of a hat, try feathers attached to a headband. Use small lines to get the feathery texture.

SHOES

Use curves to draw these smart shoes. As with men's footwear, two-tone styles were all the rage!

THE 1960S

DESIGN SOME COOL CLOTHES AND HAIRSTYLES - SIXTIES STYLE!

HAIRSTYLES

The famous men's 'mop top' style is basically a simple inverted bowl shape. For the shorter Rockabilly look, add an upturned quiff above the forehead. Use wavy lines for long hair.

TIES

Draw rows of black diamond shapes to create a trendy '60s tie. Draw bigger sets of diamonds for a more colourful design.

SHIRT FABRIC PATTERNS

Bold, colourful patterns were popular in the '60s. Recreate them using repeating curved shapes or rows of round-edged squares and rectangles.

SHOES

Footwear became bolder and more exciting in the '60s. Even men's shoes came in jazzy patterns and colours.

HATS

As hairstyles grew in the '60s, hat styles had to adapt in shape! Draw simple shapes and curves and decorate with stripes and two-tone patterns.

HAIRSTYLES

Like men, women had short and long hairstyles. Draw the 'bob' by sketching waves with small, upward curls at the end.

This typical '60s cut has more volume as the hair is swept up. Use long, wavy lines.

DRESS FABRIC PATTERNS

Geometric designs were really popular in this era. Design your own by sketching rows of circles or squares. Draw groups of overlapping 'C' shapes and paint them in bright colours for another '60s look.

SHOES AND BOOTS

Sketch tall boots and platform shoes, then add bright colours and striking patterns for the perfect '60s design!

THE 1970S

FLARES, PLATFORM SHOES AND LONG HAIR... IT'S THE SEVENTIES!

HAIRSTYLES
Men tended to have long hair in the '70s. Draw the style on the left by sketching long sweeping curves, starting from the crown. Use fewer lines to draw a neater hairstyle.

WAISTCOAT
Create a hippie-style waistcoat by adding rows of tassels and beads. Simple patterns add visual interest and earthy colours make clothing look leathery.

SHIRT PATTERNS
Shirts in the '70s were often bright and gaudy! Recreate these patterns using square, circle and triangle shapes. Place the shapes inside each other, and/or dot them about.

TROUSERS
Draw trousers with high waists and chunky belts. Use long sweeping lines to sketch flared bottoms.

SHOES
Fashionable men's shoes had thick soles. Draw them using more box-like shapes than normal shoes. Colour them with strong, contrasting tones.

HAIRSTYLES

Women's hair in the '70s was often long and straight like men's. To draw a long, wavy style, use lots of large curves and swirls, building up the different layers.

FABRIC PATTERNS

Patterns with wavy lines, swirls and flowers were big in this decade! Design some yourself using two or more bold, contrasting colours.

HATS

Hats from the '70s are easy to draw since they are basically dome-shaped. Use curved or wavy lines to sketch the brims and add bows and ribbons for visual interest.

SHOES

The tops of women's shoes tended to look more delicate than men's. When you draw them, use more curves and sharper lines. The soles can look even chunkier, and the heels a lot higher!

THE 1980s

NEON PRINTS, LEG WARMERS AND BIG HAIR - IT'S THE EIGHTIES!

HAIRSTYLES
For a mullet (short in the front, long in the back), sketch wavy lines from the centre of the head, with more behind the ears. For a mohawk, draw long, upright lines.

HATS
Draw a cap and decorate with jagged, overlapping shapes. Or, sketch a wide-brim hat shape and fill it with crosshatch shading.

SHOES
Draw small squares on a pair of pumps to create a chequered design. For trainers, use lots of random, angular shapes and make them as bright as you can!

SHIRTS AND TROUSERS
Use simple zig-zag lines for patterned '80s trousers. Sketch a sports top with a wide band across the chest. Use two or more colours that really zing!

HAIRSTYLES

Use lots of long wavy lines and 'S' shapes to recreate classic '80s big hair. Draw tiny vertical lines on the side of the head to get a shaven effect, with closely packed wavy lines for a gelled-up look.

CAPS AND BANDS

Decorate a curved hairband with zig-zags and top with a big bow in a clashing colour. Make an '80s sun visor look reflective by adding jagged highlights to it.

SHOES

Draw circles on a simple pump shape, then colour the shoes in a neon shade. Or, add zig-zags to pumps and colour in vibrant, contrasting tones.

TOPS AND SKIRTS

Draw a simple off-the-shoulder T-shirt and decorate with overlapping geometric shapes in neon colours. Use horizontal, wavy lines to draw the different layers on a ruffle skirt.

LOGOS

LOGOS GIVE BRANDS AN INSTANT IDENTITY. LEARN TO DRAW YOUR OWN LOGO – FOR A BRAND OR JUST FOR YOU!

SHAPES

THE FIRST THING TO DO IS TO PLAN THE SHAPE THAT WILL HOLD YOUR LOGO. TRY A CIRCLE, TRIANGLE, SHIELD OR EVEN STARBURST AND CUSTOMIZE THE EDGES FOR YOUR UNIQUE LOOK.

A basic shape suggests simplicity. Customize with a ribbon or a semi-circle pattern for a more ornate effect.

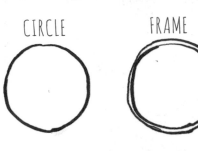

CIRCLE   FRAME   RIBBON   DECORATIVE

IMAGERY

THEN CHOOSE A FUN PICTURE OR ICON THAT MOST REPRESENTS YOU OR YOUR INTERESTS. KEEP YOUR DRAWING SIMPLE SO THAT IT IS INSTANTLY RECOGNIZABLE FROM A DISTANCE.

Most of these icons are drawn using basic shapes like circles, triangles, ovals and curved lines.

MUSICIAN   BOXER   BEST FRIEND   ANIMAL LOVER

BANNERS

NOW THINK ABOUT WHERE TO PUT THE NAME OF YOUR BRAND, IF YOU WANT TO INCLUDE IT. YOU COULD USE A BANNER TO HOLD YOUR TEXT AND COLOUR IT TO REPRESENT YOU.

Create a banner using curvy lines and triangle shapes. Add your brand name, then colour it in.

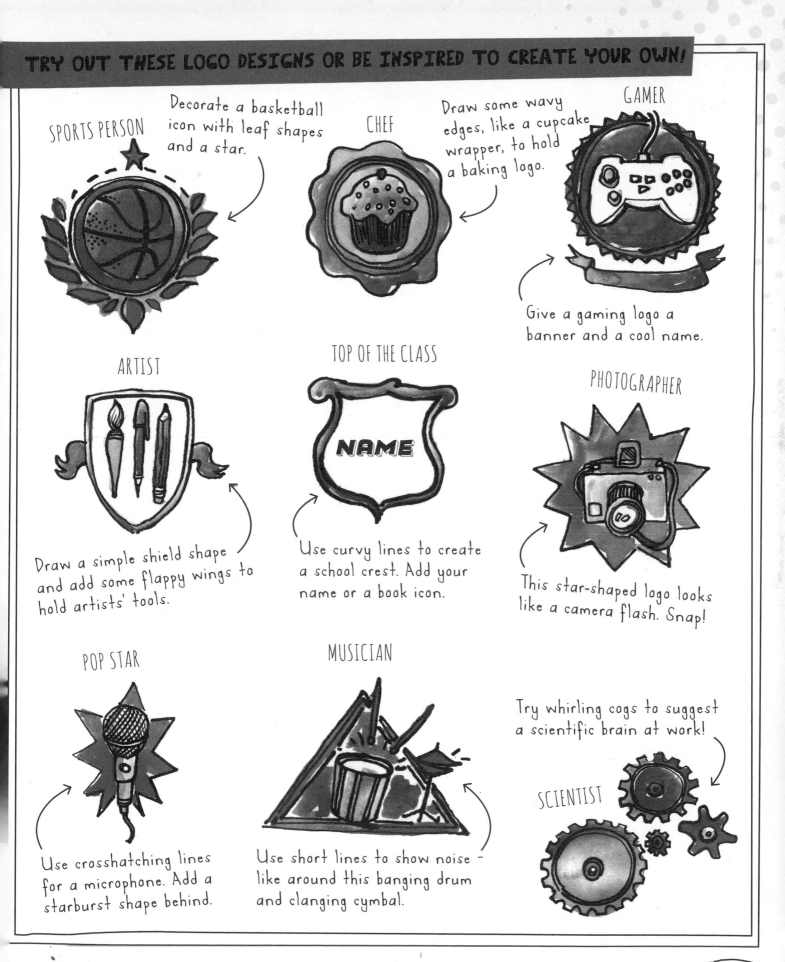

SPORTS PERSON

Decorate a basketball icon with leaf shapes and a star.

CHEF

Draw some wavy edges, like a cupcake wrapper, to hold a baking logo.

GAMER

Give a gaming logo a banner and a cool name.

ARTIST

Draw a simple shield shape and add some flappy wings to hold artists' tools.

TOP OF THE CLASS

NAME

Use curvy lines to create a school crest. Add your name or a book icon.

PHOTOGRAPHER

This star-shaped logo looks like a camera flash. Snap!

POP STAR

Use crosshatching lines for a microphone. Add a starburst shape behind.

MUSICIAN

Use short lines to show noise - like around this banging drum and clanging cymbal.

Try whirling cogs to suggest a scientific brain at work!

SCIENTIST

POP ART

1 FOR A POP ART FACE, START WITH A PHOTO OF A FACE WITH A STRONG CONTRAST BETWEEN DARK AND LIGHT AREAS. USE A PENCIL TO TRACE THE OUTLINES OF THE HEAD AND FACIAL FEATURES.

2 DRAW MORE OUTLINES ON THE FACE TO SEPARATE THE MAIN AREAS OF LIGHT AND DARK. TRY TO KEEP THESE SHAPES AS SIMPLE AS POSSIBLE.

3 LEAVE THE LIGHT AREAS WHITE, THEN USE GREY PENCILS OR PAINTS TO ADD SHADING TO THE AREAS THAT LOOK SLIGHTLY DARKER OR ARE IN SHADOW.

4 USE BLACK FOR THE DARKEST AREAS OF THE PORTRAIT, SUCH AS THE HAIR, EYEBROWS AND UPPER NECK.

5 PAINT YOUR PICTURE WITH STRONG VIBRANT COLOURS. THE SECRET IS TO CREATE A SHARP CONTRAST BETWEEN THE LIGHTEST AND DARKEST TONES. HAVE FUN EXPERIMENTING WITH DIFFERENT COLOURS AND DISCOVER WHICH COMBINATIONS WORK BEST FOR YOUR IMAGE!

ALIEN PLANET

TEST THE LIMITS OF YOUR IMAGINATION BY CREATING A WORLD FULL OF SLEEK SPACESHIPS AND AMAZING ALIENS!

1
FOR A SPACESHIP, START WITH THE BASIC SHAPE. USE A MIX OF CURVES AND STRAIGHT LINES TO DRAW THE HULL, FINS AND ROCKET BOOSTERS.

2
BUILD UP THE SURFACE DETAIL USING EXTRA LINES AND SMALL SHAPES. SHADE IN THE WINDOWS AND ADD FLAMES AT THE REAR.

3
CHOOSE A SIMPLE COLOUR SCHEME FOR YOUR SPACESHIP AND ADD HIGHLIGHTS AND SHADED AREAS TO MAKE IT LOOK 3D!

This alien ship is based on the body of a shark! Use similar sleek and smooth shapes to make your own spaceship look like it can glide through air or water!

Try combining parts of different animals to create an alien. This one is part bird, part spider and part butterfly!

1

FOR A FLYING ALIEN, START WITH BASIC SHAPES FOR THE BODY PARTS. USE STRAIGHT LINES FOR THE LIMBS AND CIRCLES FOR JOINTS.

2

FLESH OUT THE SHAPES AND ADD CURVES FOR THE MUSCLES. WORK ON THE FACIAL FEATURES, ADDING LOTS OF TEETH AND SCALES!

3

CHOOSE A COLOUR SCHEME FOR YOUR ALIEN. THIS ONE IS PAINTED IN VIVID TONES, SUGGESTING IT'S LIKE NOTHING FOUND ON EARTH!

Create alien buildings using simple shapes such as cones, cylinders and domes. Decorate with more complex shapes.

Think about how the locals look on your alien planet. Are they fierce or funny? Let your imagination run riot!

Create a strange alien landscape using watercolour washes in lots of different shades.

189

The Colosseum is a famous amphitheatre in Rome, Italy. It's not as tricky to draw as it looks! Start with a photo for reference.

1

USING A LIGHT PENCIL, SKETCH OUT THE TWO MAIN BASIC SHAPES OF THE COLOSSEUM, AS SHOWN, REFERRING TO YOUR PHOTO AS YOU GO.

2

LOOSELY DRAW HORIZONTAL LINES WITHIN THE SHAPES, CURVING THEM SLIGHTLY TO FOLLOW THE FRAME OF THE COLOSSEUM.

3

NOW ADD VERTICAL LINES TO CREATE A BASIS FOR THE WINDOWS.

4

START FILLING IN THE DETAILS. CREATE THE ARCHED SHAPE OF THE WINDOWS AND ENTRANCEWAYS, THEN ADD IN SOME BRICKWORK FOR TEXTURE AND DEFINITION.

5

GO OVER YOUR OUTLINES IN PEN AND INK, THEN RUB AWAY THE PENCIL LINES. KEEP THE LINEWORK LOOSE AND IMPERFECT TO CREATE THE FEEL OF A PARTIALLY RUINED BUILDING.

Draw jagged edges around the building to further suggest ruin and damage.

6 COLOUR WITH LIGHT WATERCOLOUR BRUSH WORK AND ADD SHADOWING IN THE WINDOWS TO CREATE DEPTH. DRAW AND PAINT SOME SMALL PEOPLE AT THE BOTTOM TO GIVE AN OVERALL IMPRESSION OF SIZE AND GRANDEUR.

DESERT ISLAND

MIX DIFFERENT TECHNIQUES TO CREATE THIS FANTASY SCENE.

Start with simple outlines for the trunks and leaves of palm trees. Use a bristly brush when you paint the leaves.

Draw a pencil outline of a raft, then go over it in ink. Don't worry if your linework looks rough – that's authentic!

Find some reference images online to help you draw different kinds of fish.

Use subtle blues and greens for the sea. Add white highlights on top to give the effect of light reflecting on the rippling water.

Draw a plane flying overhead to give the scene more of a story. What other vehicles or objects could you add?

For the shrubbery, use the end of a brush to dab greens and yellows onto the paper.

Paint the sand using different shades of beige and brown. The man and his raft are the main point of focus, so the surrounding area should be lighter to help them stand out.

How about a message-in-a-bottle in your scene? Add ink marks to make it look old, plus highlights to make the surface look like glass.

PUMPKIN PATTERNS

DRAW PUMPKINS THEN PRACTISE SPOOKY PATTERNS INSIDE. TRY THESE ON REAL PUMPKINS AT HALLOWEEN AND IMPRESS YOUR FRIENDS. MWAH-HA-HA!

1 DRAW AN OVAL THEN SKETCH ANOTHER ONE AROUND IT. ADD A TRIANGULAR SHAPE ON TOP AND GIVE IT A FLAT BASE, LIKE THIS.

2 SKETCH CURVES ONTO THE PUMPKIN SKIN AND DRAW A HAUNTED HOUSE SHAPE USING RECTANGLES AND TRIANGLES.

3 DRAW OVALS, TRIANGLES, RECTANGLES AND CYLINDERS FOR THE TREE, GHOST, DOOR AND WINDOWS, AS SHOWN.

Keep all the shapes connected to each other, so nothing floats about.

4 DRAW LINES AROUND SOME OF THE ELEMENTS OF YOUR PICTURE TO ADD DEPTH AND GIVE IT A 'CARVED OUT' EFFECT.

5 ADD SHADING TO THE STEM AND SKIN, THEN COLOUR THE PUMPKIN. MAKE THE BACKGROUND BRIGHT, AS IF THERE'S A CANDLE INSIDE.

CARVE YOUR DESIGN

SPIDER

Draw a spider shape using ovals for the body, triangular shapes for the fangs and cylinders for the long, spindly legs. Make sure the legs are touching the rest of the pumpkin.

Carve out the yellow bits to leave the spider in the pumpkin.

wITCH

Use pointy lines to draw a witch. Add a moon around her. Then join the witch's broomstick and dress to the moon so the witch stays in place when you carve out the gaps.

Carve out some bats around your main witch piece.

GRAVEYARD

Sketch a creepy graveyard with tombstones and a curved tree. Rub away the lines joining the tombstones and tree to the pumpkin.

Cut out the sections between the tree branches very carefully.

ASTRONAUT

1

SKETCH A CIRCLE FOR YOUR ASTRONAUT'S HEAD, OVALS FOR HER HANDS, AND STRAIGHT LINES FOR HER BODY, ARMS AND LEGS. DRAW AROUND YOUR GUIDELINES, AS SHOWN.

2

WORK UP THE SPACESUIT AND ADD A HELMET AND SOME GLOVES. RUB AWAY YOUR GUIDELINES FROM STEP 1.

3

FINISH THE HELMET AND HANDS, THEN CREATE CREASES IN THE SPACESUIT USING CURVED LINES.

4

GIVE YOUR ASTRONAUT A FACE AND HAIR. ADD CIRCLES ON HER TORSO AND A RECTANGULAR OXYGEN TANK ON HER BACK.

5
DRAW OXYGEN AND CARBON DIOXIDE PIPES BETWEEN THE TANK AND CIRCLES. NOW COLOUR YOUR PICTURE! ADD A SECTION OF THE MOON BELOW AND DOT WHITE PAINT IN A BLUE-BLACK SKY FOR STARS.

HOVER CAR

DESIGN YOUR VERY OWN CAR THAT FLIES THROUGH THE AIR!
HERE ARE A FEW IDEAS TO INSPIRE YOU...

BODY SHAPE

Start with the outline of your car. The bodywork is roughly a box shape, with two arches cut out from the side. It's up to you whether or not your car has a roof!

INVERTED WHEELS

Think about how your car will hover. This hover car has special wheels that change into rocket boosters - they flip downwards and the thrust lifts the vehicle into the air.

To draw a simple rocket booster, sketch a hat shape with a broad oval brim at the bottom.

Add spokes at the bottom of the rocket booster, plus any extra design details you like.

Finish off by adding lots of short, curved lines to the brim to make it look like tubing.

WINDSCREEN AND DRIVER

Draw a rectangle with curved corners for the windscreen. Build up the driver's body shape using curved lines and ovals.

Add more details to the driver, such as his hair and facial features. Add the seats!

Add the finer details. A few angled lines on the windscreen make it look like glass.

FIERY THRUST

Rocket flames make this car look really exciting. If you like, you could also draw smoke blasting out from underneath. What other cool features could your hover car have?

HEADLIGHTS

All cars need lights. This car has two big oval-shaped headlights with smaller indicator lights underneath. Make yours retro like this, or give über modern a try!

199

WRAPPING PAPER

USE PRETTY PATTERNS TO TURN ROLLS OF PLAIN PAPER INTO GORGEOUS GIFT WRAP!

ZIG-ZAGS

USE A PENCIL AND LONG RULER TO DIVIDE YOUR PAPER INTO HORIZONTAL STRIPS. DRAW ZIG-ZAGS AND DIAMOND PATTERNS BETWEEN THEM.

GO OVER YOUR DESIGN WITH WATERPROOF PENS, VARYING THE LINE THICKNESSES FOR IMPACT. THEN ADD SOME COLOUR! PURPLES AND GREENS WORK WELL TOGETHER.

CIRCLES

DIVIDE YOUR PAPER INTO LARGE SQUARES. SKETCH A CIRCLE IN EACH SQUARE AND A PATTERN IN EACH CIRCLE. DRAW DIAMOND SHAPES WHERE THE SQUARE CORNERS MEET.

PAINT THE WHOLE BACKGROUND IN A SINGLE COLOUR. WHEN IT'S DRY, PAINT THE CIRCLES AND SHAPES IN CONTRASTING COLOURS.

FESTIVE

ONCE AGAIN, DIVIDE THE PAPER INTO BIG SQUARES. ADD A TRIANGLE TO EVERY OTHER ONE. ADD MORE TRIANGLES TO EACH SHAPE, AS WELL AS SOME DECORATIONS.

PAINT THE BACKGROUND A PALE GREEN AND LEAVE TO DRY. USE DARKER SHADES FOR THE TREES, WITH CONTRASTING COLOURS FOR THE DECORATIONS.

BIRTHDAY

FIRST DRAW YOUR GRID, THEN SKETCH A CUPCAKE BASE IN EVERY OTHER SQUARE. DRAW A CURVE ON TOP OF EACH BASE. ADD CANDLES AND OTHER DETAILS.

USE A PALE WASH OVER THE WHOLE PAPER. THEN, FOR INTEREST, PICK OUT DETAILS SUCH AS THE CAKE CASES AND DECORATIONS IN DIFFERENT COLOURS.

CREATE A GIFT TAG TO MATCH YOUR DESIGNS. THEN TRY CREATING YOUR OWN PATTERNS!

3D TREASURE MAP

1 START WITH A TRAPEZIUM SHAPE (A RECTANGLE WITH THE SIDES SLANTING INWARDS). ADD RIPPED EDGES FOR AN OLDER, WORN-AND-TORN LOOK. DRAW A CURVED ISLAND SHAPE IN THE MIDDLE.

2 SKETCH RIPPLING LINES AROUND THE ISLAND FOR THE SEA. SHADE IN SOME CLIFF EDGES TO RAISE THE ISLAND OUT OF THE WATER. ADD A PATHWAY WITH A BIG 'X' AT THE END.

3

ADD MORE DETAILS, LIKE A PIRATE SHIP, TREASURE CHEST, CAVE, SEA MONSTER, MOUNTAINS AND TREES TO GIVE YOUR MAP MORE CHARACTER AND INTEREST. GET CREATIVE WITH THIS! COLOUR AND SHADE YOUR MAP.

MAP FEATURES

MOUNTAINS

Draw jagged triangle shapes. Add smaller triangles and lines inside your basic mountains, then shade them for a 3D effect.

CAVES

Start with a rough semi-cirle for the cave. Draw a smaller semi-circle for the opening. Add shading in and around the cave for depth.

PIRATE SHIP

Sketch curved lines and rectangles to create the ship, mast and flag. Add wavy water lines, and don't forget the skull and crossbones!

PALM TREES

Repeat small, upside-down trapezium shapes for the trunk. Then draw droopy, pointy leaves on top. Add shading to the trunk and leaves.

SEA MONSTER

Draw an oval-shaped head and two curved lines for the neck. Sketch semi-circles for the body, then triangles for the tail, spikes and horns. Add the eyes, mouth and water lines.

TREASURE CHEST

Start with a basic cuboid shape then draw a rectangular lid with two semi-circles on either side. Add lines to the chest for texture, and sketch circles and semi-circles for the treasure!

MERMAID

1 SKETCH CIRCLE GUIDES FOR THE HEAD AND JOINTS, STRAIGHT LINES FOR THE BODY AND ARMS, RECTANGLES FOR THE HANDS AND TRIANGLES FOR THE FISH TAIL.

2 ADD BASIC OVAL SHAPES AROUND THE ARMS, BODY AND TOP THREE SECTIONS OF THE TAIL.

Wavy lines create long, flowing hair and suggest movement under the sea.

3 DRAW AROUND YOUR GUIDELINES WITH A HEAVY, FLUID LINE. ADD HAIR, FINGERS AND A FLIPPY TAIL.

4 RUB AWAY YOUR GUIDELINES TO LEAVE YOUR BASIC MERMAID DRAWING.

5

NOW DRAW IN YOUR MERMAID'S FACIAL FEATURES AND ADD MORE DETAIL TO THE FISH TAIL.

Create the illusion of thick hair with different shades of the same colour.

6

PAINT YOUR MERMAID! ADD SIMPLE 'U' SHAPES ON HER TAIL TO CREATE FISH SCALES.

Make rocks from angular shapes and paint them in light and dark shades. Add cracks for texture.

Colourful sea life, like starfish, seashells and seaweed, add detail and interest to your picture.

205

WEREWOLF

Think of a human balancing on the balls of their feet for the leg shape.

Short lines on the hands and feet will help you position the claws in step 3.

1

SKETCH CIRCLES FOR THE HEAD, BODY, HANDS, FEET AND BODY JOINTS, AND STRAIGHT LINES FOR THE ARMS AND LEGS, AS SHOWN. ADD A RECTANGULAR-SHAPED SNOUT.

2

DRAW FLUID LINES AROUND YOUR GUIDES TO SUGGEST BULKY MUSCLES. SKETCH TWO TRIANGLES FOR EARS AND ADD IN THE MOUTH.

Guide your pencil outwards and downwards to create the fur.

3

ADD CLAWS, EYES AND A DOG-LIKE NOSE. SKETCH A SCRUFFY TAIL USING SHORT, FLICKY LINES. DRAW SMALL TRIANGLES FOR TEETH AND CURVED LINES ON THE CHEST AND KNEES. RUB AWAY THE LINES FROM STEP 1.

4

APPLY THE SAME FLICKY LINES YOU USED FOR THE TAIL TO ADD IN THE WEREWOLF'S FUR. STRAIGHT LINES ON THE FEET WILL GIVE THE IMPRESSION OF STRETCHED TENDONS. ERASE THE ROUGH LINES FROM STEP 2.

For an eerie, foggy scene, paint the background then dab away some areas using scrunched-up pieces of kitchen towel. Add a full moon and spindly trees.

5 COLOUR YOUR WEREWOLF! A SCRATCHY PAINTBRUSH IS GREAT FOR FUR. USE A SMALL, ROUND-ENDED BRUSH FOR SHORTER TUFTS. GIVE YOUR BEAST PIERCING YELLOW EYES.

Different tones of the same colour will create texture on the werewolf's fur, and on the chilly blades of grass.

COMIC STYLE

1 SKETCH PERSPECTIVE LINES TO HELP YOU DRAW A SUPERHERO COMING STRAIGHT AT YOU OUT OF THE PAGE. ADD AN OVAL SHAPE FOR THE HEAD WITH A HORIZONTAL CURVED LINE BELOW IT.

Keep things simple at this stage. Just use a few lines and shapes to help you think about the pose.

Comic style is about exaggerated elements and simple features. Once you've mastered your character, try drawing a whole comic strip!

2 DRAW THE ROUGH SHAPE OF YOUR FIGURE WITHIN YOUR GUIDES, PAYING CAREFUL ATTENTION TO THE PERSPECTIVE. THE FISTS ARE NEAR TO US SO NEED TO LOOK VERY BIG. THE LEGS AND FEET ARE FURTHER AWAY SO SHOULD APPEAR MUCH SMALLER.

3 ADD MORE DETAIL. SKETCH IN THE SHAPES OF THE HAIR AND FINGERS AND GIVE YOUR SUPERHERO A SIMPLE, SILLY COMIC EXPRESSION. TO ADD MOVEMENT, DRAW A FLOWING CAPE USING CURVED LINES.

4 USE A HEAVIER PENCIL TO ADD EVEN MORE SURFACE DETAIL AND SHADOW. GO OVER THE DRAWING IN BLACK INK, THEN PAINT YOUR SUPERHERO IN BRIGHT, COMIC-BOOK COLOURS.

Sketch extra lines and clouds to make your superhero look like he's whizzing through the air really fast!

Draw extra comic shapes using zig-zag lines and fat lettering!

WHOOSH!

ZOOM!

MOSAIC

1 START WITH A BASIC SHAPE TO BUILD YOUR MOSAIC AROUND. FOR A BUTTERFLY, SKETCH A VERTICAL LINE, THEN DRAW A SIMPLE WING ON EACH SIDE.

2 DRAW WAVY LINES AROUND THE BUTTERFLY WINGS, READY FOR THE MOSAIC PATTERN LATER ON. ADD A SEMI-CIRCULAR HEAD AND A POINT FOR THE BODY.

5 RUB AWAY ANY PENCIL MARKS THEN COLOUR YOUR MOSAIC. KEEP YOUR BUTTERFLY'S COLOURS SYMMETRICAL BUT DECORATE THE REST OF THE MOSAIC IN A MORE FLUID WAY TO HELP THE BUTTERFLY STAND OUT.

3 SKETCH A SYMMETRICAL PATTERN ON THE WINGS AND A MIXTURE OF SHAPES AROUND THE BUTTERFLY. THESE DON'T NEED TO MIRROR EACH OTHER.

4 DRAW THE INDIVIDUAL MOSAIC PIECES USING TINY RECTANGLES, SQUARES, CIRCLES AND TRIANGLES. GO OVER YOUR OUTLINES WITH AN INK PEN.

PILOT

Use stars, circles and wing shapes to design your own air force badges.

1

DRAW AN OVAL FOR THE HEAD. ADD HORIZONTAL AND VERTICAL CURVES AS GUIDELINES, AS SHOWN. DRAW A CURVED SHAPE FOR THE SHOULDERS.

2

GIVE THE SHOULDERS A BIT MORE SHAPE AND SKETCH IN THE OUTLINE OF THE HELMET. ADD A CURVED SHAPE FOR THE CHIN.

3

USING YOUR GUIDELINES, SKETCH IN THE FACIAL ELEMENTS – NOSE, MOUTH AND SUNGLASSES. ADD LINES FOR THE SHOULDER STRAPS.

4

REFINE YOUR PENCIL LINES AND CARRY ON ADDING DETAIL TO THE FACE AND STRAPS. DRAW A ROUNDED-OFF TRIANGULAR SHAPE FOR THE FACE MASK.

5

NOW ADD THE FINER DETAILS. DRAW SMALL CIRCLES AND LINES ON THE HELMET AND SKETCH AN EARPIECE ON ONE SIDE. ADD TUBING AND OTHER DETAILS TO THE FACE MASK.

As you add more detail, rub out any guidelines that you don't need any more.

Use lots of tiny curved shapes to create the texture of tubing.

6 DRAW THE SHAPES OF THE SEAT AND PLANE, THEN GO OVER YOUR DRAWING WITH AN INK PEN. ADD EXTRA LINES HERE AND THERE TO SHOW THE SHADED AREAS AND TO CREATE MORE SURFACE TEXTURE. FINALLY, COLOUR IN YOUR PILOT AND HIS PLANE.

Use a light shade of blue for the sky. To create clouds, wash away painted areas with a clean brush.

Decide which direction the light is coming from and work out which areas will look lighter and which will appear darker.

EGYPT

LEARN TO DRAW THE ELEMENTS OF ANCIENT EGYPT AND DRAW LIKE AN EGYPTIAN!

HIEROGLYPHICS: Ancient Egyptians used pictures of objects, people and animals as a writing system. Draw bold, black lines and curves to create your own hieroglyphs.

ANCIENT EGYPTIAN WOMAN: Try drawing this figure with long, smooth lines. Use a limited colour palette of bright yellows, oranges and blues to give your painting authenticity.

SPHINX: Draw this human-lion hybrid statue in bold, simple lines. Keep the facial features simple, using curved lines for the eyes, nose and mouth.

Colour your sphinx with a mix of yellow watercolour and yellow ochre for a sandy, desert-like wash. Add a bit of brown shading to give your picture more depth.

PYRAMIDS: Draw three triangle tops and add a diagonal line in each one, from the peak to the base, for a 3D feel. Add lines to suggest rough edges and the occasional stone.

Colour your pyramids in a similar way to the sphinx. Add brown shading on one side of each pyramid.

Find photos of Egyptology online or in books to help inspire your drawings!

WEDDING DRESS

1 SKETCH GUIDELINES FOR THE HEAD, ARMS, SHOULDERS, TORSO AND BOUQUET. USE A ZIG-ZAG FOR A POSE WITH PERSONALITY. THEN DRAW THE OUTLINE OF THE DRESS.

2 FLESH OUT THE SHAPES OF THE HEAD, SHOULDERS, ARMS AND HANDS. ADD THE BRIDE'S HAIR AND SKETCH THE UPPER PART OF HER DRESS WITH CURVED LINES.

Add a rough patch of colour to make the pale dress stand out.

3

USE LONG, SWEEPING CURVES FOR THE VEIL. DRAW THE FLOWERS AND USE WAVY LINES TO SKETCH THE RIBBONS. RUB OUT GUIDELINES.

4 PAINT THE DRESS A PALE COLOUR, ADDING DARKER TONES FOR THE SHADOWY AREAS. PAINT THE BRIDE'S SKIN AND HAIR AND USE A BRIGHT COLOUR FOR THE FLOWERS.

DESIGN A DRESS

Create your own wedding dress designs by experimenting with different shapes, patterns and textures.

Dab the end of your brush on to the paper to give this faint, stippled texture.

Choose a simple motif and repeat it all over the dress to create an elegant pattern. Keep the colours simple and feminine.

Roses are easy to draw. They're just groups of rough-edged circles painted pink.

For an original look, add an accessory in an eye-catching colour.

Add extra details to the hem of your dress for that finishing touch. You could add a simple coloured border, or draw layers of wavy lines for a more dramatic look.

Draw lots of overlapping bands to create this beautiful bow!

ILLUSIONS

IT'S FUN BREAKING THE RULES OF PERSPECTIVE TO CREATE IMPOSSIBLE OBJECTS. YOU CAN EVEN CREATE PICTURES THAT LOOK LIKE THEY'RE MOVING!

IMPOSSIBLE OVAL

1 USING A PENCIL, SKETCH A HORIZONTAL GUIDELINE. THEN DRAW AN ARC ON EITHER SIDE TO FORM A SYMMETRICAL OVAL SHAPE.

2 ADD A LARGER CURVE ATTACHED TO ONE END OF THE OVAL. DRAW ANOTHER CURVE UNDERNEATH, ATTACHED TO THE OPPOSITE END.

3 DRAW A LARGER OVAL AROUND ALL THE SHAPES YOU'VE SKETCHED SO FAR. LOOK CLOSELY AT THE PICTURE BELOW FOR ITS POSITION.

4 GO OVER YOUR DRAWING WITH A WATERPROOF PEN. TRY VARYING THE LINE THICKNESSES TO CREATE A MORE 3D EFFECT OVERALL.

5 ADD COLOUR WITH WATERCOLOUR INKS. MAKE ONE SIDE DARKER THAN THE OTHER TO ADD TO THE 3D FEEL. YOUR DRAWING IS DONE, BUT THE CRAZY THING IS THIS OBJECT CAN'T ACTUALLY EXIST - LOOK HOW IT TWISTS!

THE FAKE FORK

Using a soft pencil, draw a simple rectangular shape as a guide.

Add diagonal lines to the rectangle to start creating a box shape that looks 3D.

Draw a parallel horizontal line at the bottom and a short slanted vertical one. Add extra lines to create a big 'C' shape.

Sketch extra lines in the middle of the 'C' shape to add extra depth. Rub out the guideline on the right-hand side.

Draw a cylinder shape at the end of each pair of lines. Add colour, but notice how the middle and bottom poles come from nowhere!

HYPNOTIZER

Draw a large cross with a ruler. Using the central point as a guide, draw two circles with a pair of compasses.

Add three more circles as shown, keeping the point of the compass at the same central point.

Using your ruler again, draw six lines across the diameter of the big circle. You should now have 12 triangular segments.

Colour alternating sections in black. Stare hard and watch the shapes move!

INDEx

ABOUT THE ARTISTS

TALENTED ARTISTS FROM AROUND THE WORLD HAVE CONTRIBUTED THEIR SKILLS AND ILLUSTRATIONS TO THIS BOOK!

PAULA FRANCO is a children's book illustrator and graphic designer. She enjoys creating new characters and detailed backgrounds. Paula lives in Argentina with her two rescue dogs, Mora (which means 'blackberry' in spanish) and Mizzy.

SI CLARK is an illustrator and animator. He grew up in the countryside but now lives in London. He started drawing at a very early age and has pretty much been drawing every day since then. Si is obsessed with drawing trees and cities, as well as finding strange textures to scan into his drawings!

YASUKO has developed a graphic illustration style, mixing ink work, brush strokes and digital textures. She loves Japanese fashion and sometimes makes her own clothes. Yasuko lives and works in Paris and loves to spend time drawing in the Louvre art museum.

ALEX HEDWORTH works as an illustrator for an animation studio. He has been drawing for as long as he can remember – his first drawings were copies of comic books and he is now working on a graphic novel of his own.

JULIE INGHAM is an illustrator and designer who lives and works by the sea in West Sussex, England. Her favourite things to draw are skyscrapers and all things decorative!

TOM MCGRATH'S work is inspired by artwork he has seen, books he has read, films he has watched and even on occasion by real life. He is obsessed by clouds, fish and airships.

STEVE HORROCKS was born in Merseyside, England. He now lives in California with his wife, where he works at a major feature animation studio and continues to pursue his passion for creating art at a personal level too.

DAVID SHEPHARD is a children's book illustrator and designer. He lives in the shadow of a Norman castle in Sussex, England, with his wife, children and several pets. He loves drawing people and faces and works best in his attic, where his family slides his dinners under the door!

now go make your mark!

You know the materials. You know the techniques.
You've mastered fashion, patterns, people and even aliens.

So go sketch, practise, doodle and draw these ideas and more...

And go DRAW IT ALL!